Thomas Somerville

Am I my Brother's Keeper?

and other sermons

Thomas Somerville

Am I my Brother's Keeper?
and other sermons

ISBN/EAN: 9783337264642

Printed in Europe, USA, Canada, Australia, Japan

Cover: Foto ©Lupo / pixelio.de

More available books at **www.hansebooks.com**

Sermons and Lectures

ON SPECIAL OCCASIONS.

BLACKFRIARS PARISH CHURCH,
WESTERCRAIGS.

AM I MY BROTHER'S KEEPER?

AND OTHER SERMONS.

BY

REV. THOMAS SOMERVILLE, A.M.,

BLACKFRIARS PARISH CHURCH.

𝕲𝖑𝖆𝖘𝖌𝖔𝖜 :

R. ROBERTSON, 304 DUKE STREET, DENNISTOUN.

TO MY FRIENDS

IN

ST. JAMES'S, GLASGOW;

ST. ANDREW'S, BRITISH COLUMBIA;

ST. DAVID'S, KIRKINTILLOCH;

AND

BLACKFRIARS,

THESE SERMONS AND LECTURES WHICH THEY HEARD
ARE DEDICATED WITH AFFECTIONATE RESPECT.

BLACKFRIARS PARISH,
GLASGOW, *November, 1894.*

I HAVE yielded to the solicitation of some friends who desire to have some of the sermons, which they heard, in more permanent form. Sermons are made for preaching, not reading; and it is seldom that those who have heard them gladly read them with much interest. I will rejoice if they are well received and do good.

I have also added a few lectures, which have always been a part of our service in St. Andrew's, British Columbia; Kirkintilloch, and Blackfriars.

THOMAS SOMERVILLE.

CONTENTS.

AM I MY BROTHER'S KEEPER? 9
  "Am I my brother's keeper?"—*Gen. iv. 9.*

THEY MEASURE THEMSELVES BY THEMSELVES, . . 19
  "They measuring themselves by themselves, and comparing themselves among themselves, are not wise."—*2 Cor. x. 12.*

HAST THOU FOUND ME, O MINE ENEMY? . . . 28
  "Hast thou found me, O mine enemy?"—*1 Kings xxi. 20.*

WORK OUT YOUR OWN SALVATION, ... 35
  "Work out your own Salvation with fear and trembling, for it is God which worketh in you, both to will and to do of His good pleasure."—*Phil. ii. 12, 13.*

BE STRONG: QUIT YOU LIKE MEN, ... 43
  "Be strong: quit you like men."—*1 Cor. xvi. 13.*

MY SOUL CLEAVETH TO THE DUST, ... 49
  "My soul cleaveth to the dust: but quicken thou me, according to Thy word."—*Psalms cxix. 25.*

GROW IN GRACE, ... 58
  "Grow in grace, and in the knowledge of our Lord and Saviour Jesus Christ."—*2 Peter iii. 18.*

BEHOLD! I STAND AT THE DOOR AND KNOCK, . . 68
  "Behold I stand at the door and knock, if any man will hear My voice and open the door, I will come in to him, and will sup with him, and he with Me."—*Rev. iii. 20.*

THE LORD IS GREAT, ... 74
  "The Lord is great and greatly to be praised."—*Psalms xcvi. 4.*

He Knew what was in Man, ... 80
    "He knew what was in man."—*John ii. 25.*

He that Ruleth his Spirit, ... 86
    "He that ruleth his spirit is better than he that taketh a city.—*Proverbs xvi. 32.*

And Thou Shalt be Missed, ... 93
    "And thou shalt be missed, because thy seat is empty."—*1 Sam. xx. 18.*

Faith, Hope, Charity, ... 101
    "Now abideth faith, hope, charity, but the greatest of these is charity."—*1 Cor. xiii. 13.*

The Puzzle of the Poor, ... 108
    "Thou, O God, hast prepared of Thy goodness for the poor." *Psalms lxviii. 10.*

The Puzzle of the Rich, ... 117
    "Charge them that are rich in this world, that they be not high-minded, nor trust in uncertain riches, but in the living God, who giveth us richly all things to enjoy."—*1 Tim. vi. 17.*

A Foolish King, ... 127
    1 Kings xii.

The Temple of Solomon, ... 135
    "Thus all the work that Solomon made for the house of the Lord was finished."—*1 Kings vii. 51.*

The Elect Lady, ... 142
    2 John i. 1.

Address on Leaving Old College Church, . . 149

AM I MY BROTHER'S KEEPER?

"AM I MY BROTHER'S KEEPER?"—*Genesis iv. 9.*

(*Preached in St. Andrew's Parish Church, May, 1873, by request of the Committee of College Parish Church.*)

HERE we find—*first*,—A good question asked in a bad spirit; *second*,—The true answer to that question; *third*,—We consider the prevalence of this Cain spirit; *fourth*,—The true cure of this Cain spirit.

I.—A GOOD QUESTION ASKED IN A BAD SPIRIT.

The history of our race opens with the page of innocence, but it is soon stained with the blood of transgression. The first that was a son became the first that was a murderer. We can conceive the joy which our great ancestors had at first in their children. In them they beheld the partial fulfilment of the great promise, that "the seed of the woman should bruise the head of the serpent." When they heard their voices, and watched their boyish gambols upon the lea, they looked forward with hope to the future. But, alas! a cloud soon gathered upon that early home. With grief they marked that their eldest boy had a violent temper, and that he was not only hasty with his word, but often hasty with his hand. As time went on, this violence manifested at first towards his younger brother, bursts forth upon his parents. He that has been a cruel brother proves an undutiful, rebellious son. He turns from them with the sour look and the sullen word; and in still riper youth he becomes impious and profane. He asks in sneering tones concerning God and truth and duty. He refuses to accompany them on the Sabbath mornings to the altar upon the plain, to render there their grateful orisons to God Almighty. His dark soul is filled with doubt, and with envy at the peace of others. An old writer has said: "There never was an envy that was not bloody: if it do not take your neighbour's life, it will take your own." The worst thing about sin is, that it never comes to anyone at first in its big, black, ugly form. It never approaches bearing in its hand the full cup of misery it surely mixes for its victims. It steals upon us slowly and imperceptibly like the noiseless shades of evening, or the rising tides of ocean. The guide has often ascended yonder snow-clad mountain, and on every occasion made dangerous efforts—and always with impunity. His fame has gone forth to the nations. But one day, in doing that which he had often done before, he loses foothold on the slippery ice, and is plunged, a broken, bruised mass, into the crevasse underneath. So is it with every sinful and vicious habit. From bad to worse it leads its victim on, until it plunges him into the pit of destruction. It was thus with Cain. Through all the separate stages of cruelty to a younger brother, undutifulness to his parents, impiety towards God, envy and malice, had he come, until now he stretches forth his hand to murder. Often had that hand fallen heavily upon his brother's form ere the fatal blow was struck. At length, one day, when they were in the open field together, a rush of frenzied envy came upon his soul, and he felled his brother to the earth. But the effect of that blow soon changed his envy to alarm. For there he beheld before him that which is still terrible to us all—death—the first death. He had only heard of it before as the threatened punishment of transgression. His heart sickens, and he recoils from it; but he cannot tear himself away. Turning, and touching the bleeding garments, he says:

> What is this? 'Tis wet, and yet there are no dews.
> Ah, me! 'Tis blood, my blood; my brother's and my own,
> And taken by me! Oh! what have I further to do with life,
> Since I have taken life from my own flesh?
> But he cannot be dead. Is silence death?
> I will speak to him, and what shall I say? My brother?
> Ah, no! He will not answer to that name,
> For brethren smite not each other.
> . . . . Yet speak to me.
> Oh, for one word from that gentle voice,
> That I may learn to hear my own again!

Not long, however, do these softer feelings retain possession of his heart. The force of habit is terrible. The old, bad spirit comes back upon him. Abel's blood cries to God in heaven, and God in heaven speaks to Cain upon the earth: "Where is Abel thy brother?" And what is his reply in the hour when you would have expected expressions of sorrow and remorse, if not repentance? Turning his face to the Majesty of Heaven, he sourly and indignantly says: "I know not. Am I my brother's keeper?"

II.—The true answer to that question.

The question was uttered in the open field, and we can conceive the rocks around echoing back: "Brother's keeper!" At all events, God gave answer to Cain, and answers us in emphatic form.

Thy brother's keeper art thou—ordained by that Mighty Being, in whose hand thy breath is, and whose are all thy ways. The few members of that first family have become as many millions, scattered over the face of the wide world; but yet, wherever they are, they are all united as bearers of the same common nature, partakers of the same common bounty, sharers of the same common frailty, and as bound by the same common interest. That was a good word which Cromwell applied to his Government of our country when he called it—not Republic, nor Empire, but the Commonwealth of Great Britain. And so the round world is just one great commonwealth in which the good or the evil of one is the good or evil of all. None of us liveth for himself. The individual lives for his family, the family for the community, the community for the nation, and all for God. You cannot take from the shore of the inland harbour a single cupful of water without creating an effect, sure if imperceptible, upon the furthest confines of the great ocean itself; and so you can neither hurt nor help a single individual without affecting all humanity thereby. Every virtuous act, every true word, adds to the common stock of goodness, as every vicious act, every false word, adds to the common stock of badness; and we influence our neighbour not so much by those words cautiously spoken, and those actions deliberately done, as by our ordinary life from day to day, and the words that fall from us without thought. The stone was flung by careless hand into the waters of the lake beneath, and was lost to sight. But that was not all; for mark the eddying circles that form around, and roll away out to the very shore. So also that word of scorn or hate flung from your lips in casual company, or that action lightly done without thought of observation, has become a poisonous influence in the heart of another. This is a terrible power which we bear about with us—this of influencing each other for good or evil by all we do. It was born with us; it has strengthened with our strength; it has become bone of our bone, and flesh of our flesh. We cannot cast it from us. It is our moral shadow, irrevocable and eternal. Every day and every way are we keepers of our brethren; every day we are either Abels speaking righteousness, or Cains destroying good.

III.—WE CONSIDER THE PREVALENCE OF THIS CAIN SPIRIT

Ever since sin entered the world this wretched, selfish spirit has had its manifestations. All through the ages there have been those who ignored this responsibility for the keeping of their brother. We need not go back for illustrations to the antediluvian times and their rampant violence; nor to the barbaric ages, when "man's inhumanity to man made countless thousands mourn;" nor to those mighty conquerors who, in their ambitious passion, have hewn down men, as reapers the golden grain upon the harvest-field. We need not point to those dark dungeons, in which have perished some of the best and bravest of our race; nor to the fierce persecutions that have been waged against the most worthy. We need not go abroad to the heathen world, nor to those lands where slavery exists. In every land and in every sphere of society we will find it, even within the pale of the Christian Church. Look around you upon that man whom a beneficent Creator has endowed with health and wealth. Within his mansion are gathered all that can please the eye or the ear. He is a man of taste, of intelligence, and comparative purity. And, yet, there he sits at the window of his mansion looking out upon the eddying currents of human life, all unheeding. Never was the widow's heart made glad by him. Never were the orphan's hands raised to bless him. The waters of evil may rage around, and bear away thousands in their fury; but what cares he so long as he and his, sitting upon their little island, are not endangered? What is this man doing by his life and conversation but re-echoing the cry of Cain, "Am I my brother's keeper?"

What of ourselves? Are we faithful in this matter of keeping our brother? Are we true soldiers in the army of the Lord, contending always for that which is good? Are we diligent labourers in the goodly vineyard he has given us to cultivate? What has been our influence upon the community and upon those around us? Have we remembered our brother for good on life's highway?

"Where is thy brother?" God said that day to Cain. Where is thy brother? God says this day to us. Where is that brother with whom you started on life's journey, who early fell by the way, and was wrecked without one warning word, without one helping hand from you? He is gone long ago from the ranks of the living. His blood cries to God against you. Where is that sister that was brought under your influence—perhaps as a domestic into your home—the girl that might have been saved by your kindly sympathy and your prudent dealing, but who, alas! received them not? Where is thy sister? Crushed as an unclean thing by the wayside. In her sin and her shame she testifies against you.

There are sad memories stirred up within us all by such a question as this. I remember one at college, one who had within him the sparkling light of genius, one who could write with ease that which found its place in the best literature of the day, but also one who was tied down by intemperate habits. He died, and was followed by some of us to the graveyard amid the old streets of our city. When we returned to the wretched place which he had called his home, we found a few old papers scribbled over, one of them with these words, which in all my wanderings I have never forgotten—they are so sad and reproachful:

> Oh God! how often had I turned to Thee
> With a new soul, and kept my heel

> Upon the form of conquered sin;
> But that, turning round, the world my purpose smote
> With a sore buffet on the bleeding brow;
> And scared Repentance left me with a shriek,
> Closing heaven's gates behind her as she passed.

How often do we smite with a sore buffet on the bleeding brow those who are turning round in their agony appealing for our aid!

IV.—THE TRUE CURE FOR THIS CAIN SPIRIT.

The true and only cure for this is the Spirit of our God and Saviour Jesus Christ. There can only be a real union among men in so far as they participate in a common spirit. In things physical there can only be union where there is a common affinity. The atoms of a sand-heap are close enough together, but they are not united; and so men may be close enough together, but unless they have a common spirit, they will not be united. This is the only true basis for union. Men have tried other things, such as power, organisation, and have failed. Alexander the Great forced different nations and races into one great empire which was the glory of the age; but there was no common spirit, and upon his death it was split up into fragments. The very hugeness of an organisation is often the cause of weakness and failure. How powerful, on the other hand, is a common spirit to unite men! Look at our own country, how many different classes there are in it. Sometimes the political and ecclesiastical controversies cause fear; but let a foreign foe threaten to set foot upon our land, and all come lovingly together to repel the invader, moved by the common spirit of love to the country and the Constitution. Such a union does Christ propose to form in Himself by the infusion of His own spirit. As men get nearer to Him they get nearer to one another. And what is His spirit? It is the spirit of love, the spirit of sacrifice for worthy ends, the spirit of true righteousness. Look at Him when He was upon the earth, how He was ever ready to save the lost, to heal the sick, to comfort the mourner, to pour out His soul unto the death! He died, the just for the unjust, to bring us to God. He was the Saviour and the Friend of man. That Sacrifice has taken the world by the heart. The Spirit of God taketh the things that are Christ's and sheweth them unto us. Thus it becomes "the power of God unto salvation to every one that believeth." "He humbled Himself, and became obedient unto death — even the death of the Cross." "*Wherefore*," we read, "God hath exalteth Him, and given Him a name that is above every name." What is that *name?* Not certainly the name of power, although that also is His, but the name of LOVE. It is His glory, not that He can send the shafts of His power further than the furthest rolling orb, but that He can still bend on earth the brother's eye, still reach down the helping hand and pardon and bless—and pardon and bless, and save unto the uttermost all that come unto God by Him. That is the spirit of Christ; and that is the true cure for our wretched, selfish, Cain-like spirit that is ever ready to say, "Am I my brother's keeper?"

THEY MEASURE THEMSELVES BY THEMSELVES.

"THEY MEASURING THEMSELVES BY THEMSELVES, AND COMPARING THEMSELVES AMONG THEMSELVES, ARE NOT WISE."
—*2 Cor. x. 12.*

(*Preached in St. David's, Kirkintilloch, 1871.*)

THE Apostle was writing to the Church at Corinth—a Grecian city. These Greeks had long idolized the beautiful in Nature and in human form. Corinth was an expression of this, with its two beautiful bays sweeping up to the gates, the temple-crowned summit of Acro-Corinthus, and the graceful statues that everywhere adorned the streets. It was difficult for them to rise above this mode of thought, and to realize how immensely superior was that which was morally beautiful. The Apostle Paul was, in bodily presence, an offence to them. We often picture Paul as a man of majestic mien and powerful voice. This was not the case. So far as we can learn from Scripture or tradition, he was small of stature, partially lame, partially blind, and his voice weak and harsh. These physical defects were a thorn in the flesh. He lamented deeply that he had not the aid of natural powers to recommend the truth of God. He compared unfavourably with the other teachers of philosophy in Corinth. He had nothing of their pleasing presence. Whilst resident among the Corinthians he had wrought at tentmaking, and was altogether too plain for their liking. Comparing themselves with themselves, they were not wise enough to appreciate the truth apart from the appearance of the teacher. But not only in bodily presence, but in speech was he an offence to them. There was nothing of the sophistry and varied climaxes of the orators of the Porch and of the Grove. In the *Church* there would be certainly a better tone of feeling than in the *city* of Corinth. The polished block retains much of the grit and colour of the native quarry from which it is taken; and so also the Corinthian Church reflected too much the spirit of the Corinthian world. In their ecclesiastical gossip they had been led to speak lightly of him: "His letters are weighty and powerful; but his bodily presence is weak and his speech contemptible." And the Apostle's heart struck fire at this. He proudly writes: "Do you look on things after the outward appearance? If any man trust to himself that he is Christ's, let him of himself think this again, that, as he is Christ's, even so we are Christ's;" and then follows this touch of delicate, yet severe sarcasm. They had accused him of a want of boldness—*i.e.*, of personal presence; and he replies: "I am not bold enough for some things. I am not bold enough to do that which many amongst you do, who look complacently upon themselves and undervalue all others." "We dare not make ourselves of the number, or compare ourselves with some who commend themselves: for they measuring themselves by themselves, and comparing themselves among themselves, are not wise."

It is not wise to compare ourselves among ourselves, or judge ourselves by ourselves.

First,—It is not wise, because it induces self-satisfaction with small attainments; *second,*—Because it deprives us of the instruction we may receive from those better than ourselves; *third,*—Because it ignores the ground of Christian effort and the standard of Christian progress—Christ Himself.

I.—IT IS NOT WISE, BECAUSE IT LEADS TO SELF-SATISFACTION WITH SMALL ATTAINMENTS.

Narrow-mindedness is proverbially contemptible. The man who has lived in some small circle is always ill-informed and conceited. Ignorant of the great world beyond him, he is ever ready to urge his own opinion against the whole world. You will find him more positive in his assertions than the statesman who has controlled the destiny of a great nation, or the ripe scholar who has devoted his life to learning And why? Just because he has always been dealing with those beneath him, or on the same level, and hence acquired a self-satisfaction which makes him narrow in his sympathies, but ready to give judgment on all.

The young man just starting on life's journey is often confident and headstrong. To him all his fathers have been fools. He goes forth and takes his place with others in the race of life, and he changes. He comes to have a healthy respect for those he formerly despised. He discovers a virtue in many things he formerly contemned, and becomes indifferent to some things he formerly deemed of infinite importance. It is still more the case if he goes away from his native place. As Dr. Johnson has said: "All travel has its advantages. If a man sees better countries, he may learn to improve his own; if fortune carries him to worse, he may learn to enjoy his own."

So also with the Church that ignores all others. There is engendered a spiritual conceit which, scarcely tolerant in itself, is rashly intolerant towards others. See those Pharisees of old, how they narrowed down all religion to that of their own small form. How complacently they boasted of their schools of Hillel and Shammai; how contentedly they rested in their dogmas and little round of ceremonies!

Comparing themselves among themselves, they became utterly blinded to all goodness which was not of their form; judging themselves by themselves, they shut themselves out from healthy influences. All heart and soul fled from them. Instead of humanizing and exalting, they dried up the springs of true life. Religion, by revealing a God infinitely high and holy, should make men humble; but these men had become intoxicated with spiritual pride. Religion should make men charitable; for he who sees how lofty a thing true goodness is, will reserve his severest censures for himself; but these men were censorious beyond all example. Religion, which proclaims the loving-kindness of God, should enlarge the circle of our sympathies; but they indulged a pitiable exclusiveness which was ever on the watch for the smallest possible answer to the question: "Who is my neighbour?" Religion, sweeping down from Heaven with Heaven's mercy, should come with its hopes and its consolations to the poor, the ignorant, and the forlorn; but these men, instead of smoothing for the multitude the way to God, had rendered it all but impassable. Bound hand and foot to a little narrow system, they even rejected the Saviour because He did not conform Himself to it; they were irritated at His demand for a personal love and a real surrender of the soul to God, and moved the mob to crucify the Lord of life.

The same cause has been always attended by the same results. Exclusiveness has led to blindness and bigotry. Had the Church of Rome regarded the advancing intelligence of the people, she might still have been our Mother Church. "Come to my help against Luther," wrote Pope Adrian to his old schoolfellow Erasmus. "I cannot come to your Holiness," he replied. "The world has been besotted with ceremonies. Miserable monks have ruled all; entangling men's consciences for their own benefit. Mark this: If monks and theologians think only of themselves, no good will come of it. Look rather into the causes of all this confusion, and apply your remedies there. Send for the best and wisest men of Christendom, and take their advice." Adrian, however, rejected this advice. The Church was deaf to the cry of a people long oppressed, and hence the Reformation.

II.—It is not wise, for it deprives us of the instruction we may receive from those better than ourselves.

It is good to advise a young man to seek the company of those better than himself. Their superiority will stimulate his effort. He will unconsciously become partaker of their nature. He will grow up to them. Hence the superlative value of all good biographies. These indefinitely enlarge the circle of our experience, and give us the opportunity of coolly considering the events of life, apart from the disturbing associations that affect our own lives. By these are we taken out into the company of the good and the great, and enabled to compare ourselves with the mighty ones of our race. Our knowledge, as well as our sympathies, will thus be indefinitely enlarged. He that looks around upon his small estate in some narrow valley has but a limited view of this great world, and may think himself a person of great importance; but let him ascend the neighbouring hill, and the horizon widens out around him, and lands not his own are brought to view. Let him climb to the summit of the lofty mountain, and how wide the prospect that opens out before him. The domain beyond him appears broader and greater, until his own estate seems an insignificant herb plot. The higher we rise, either in the intellectual or the spiritual realm, the more humbly will we carry ourselves.

Our own attainment will appear lamentably little compared to that which stretches away beyond us. Thus, as Sir William Hamilton has said: "All knowledge is oscillation between two poles of ignorance. We begin with unconscious ignorance; we end with conscious ignorance." The more we know, the more we know we have to know. Therefore will those who know most make the least of it. The branches most heavily laden with fruit bend lowest to the ground. The higher the flight of the eagle in the air, the deeper the reflection in the lake beneath.

But not only do we learn humility: we actually receive of their greatness, intellectual or spiritual. In the presence of the pure we become pure. From those wiser than ourselves we catch the contagion of improvement. An eminent writer has said: "It is observed in old couples, or in persons who have lived long together, that they grow alike; and, if they should live long enough, we should not be able to know them apart. The like assimilation goes on between men of the same town, of the same sect, of the same political party. The ideas of the time are in the air, and infect all who breathe it. Now Nature abhors all such agglutinations which threaten to melt the whole world into a lump, and hastens to break them up. We learn of our contemporaries what they know, without effort, and almost through the pores of the skin. But we stop where they stop: very hardly can we make one step in advance. The great, or such as transcend fashions by their fidelity to universal ideas, save us from these federal errors. A foreign greatness is the best antidote for Cabalism."

Interchange ventilates our minds and lets them grow Just as soon as an individual, or a class, or a country lock themselves up by themselves they cease to grow—nay, they go backward, and die. Look, for instance, at the Chinese.

Having attained a high civilization, they shut themselves in. Their great wall has been a curse, rather than a blessing. God's providence is against all monopoly of knowledge. If the attempt be made to keep it in, it will take wings and fly away. Cooped up and kept close, it will wither and die. Circulate it, and it will expand; scatter it, and it will abound. It is increased by travelling up and down among the sympathies of those whose hearts love it, whose natures crave it, and whose abilities reproduce and multiply it. Cadmus bore the letters from Egypt to Greece, and these few letters became a literature; Augustine followed Hengist and Horsa into Britain with the elements of Christian knowledge, and how vastly they have been increased! All spiritual blessings, all cheering influences, are eminently social. They ask for companionship; they spread by contact; they are enhanced by expression; they are multiplied by free communication. Caste, which was in India the attempted enshrinement of some one virtue or some special kind of knowledge, has been the great obstacle to progress. Comparing themselves among themselves, and judging themselves by themselves, they are not wise.

III.—It is not wise, for it ignores the ground of Christian effort and the standard of Christian progress.

I can conceive of no frame of mind more inimical to the spirit of the Gospel, less willing to fall in with its merciful provisions, than this. Poverty of spirit is the condition of entrance into Christ's kingdom. A man must see himself as he is in the light of the law of God—naked, and blind, and miserable—before he will prostrate himself before the Redeemer. Comparing himself with those around him, he will be self-satisfied and indifferent. Comparing himself with the perfect law of God, he will appear lamentably deficient. Then will arise from his heart the earnest cry for mercy, which will ensure the answer of peace. The apostle who could say that, as touching the righteousness which is in the law, he was blameless, also said that he counted all things but loss "that he might win Christ and be found in Him, not having his own righteousness, which is of the law, but that which is through the faith of Christ." We must go out of ourselves to be found in Him. We in Christ, and Christ in us; this is the true ground of all Christian effort. Christ the mainspring, Christ the end, and Christ the reward of all our work.

And not only is Christ the ground of Christian effort; He is the standard of Christian excellence. With Him are we to compare ourselves; by Him are we to prove ourselves, "till we all come in the unity of the faith, and of the knowledge of the Son of God unto a perfect man, unto the measure of the stature of the fulness of Christ." The Apostle speaks of us running the race, laying aside every weight that we may run it; and, he adds, "looking unto Jesus, the author and the finisher of our faith." Christ is our mark, the perfect standard of God; and when we look to that life of sinless holiness, that life of unruffled patience, how miserably short do we find ourselves! aye, and the further we go, we will be ever reaching forth unto Him. "Christian life is like one of those problems in mathematics that can never be exactly answered. All you attain is an approximation. You may labour on for years and never reach the result. Yet your labour is not in vain. Every figure you add makes the fraction nearer by the million millionth." When I was young the skies appeared so near that I fancied I could almost touch them at yonder point where they met the earth, but with advancing years, their lofty dome receded, and became broader and grander than then ever I dreamed of; and so also at one time I thought I had mastered the whole system of theology; but truth expanded beyond system and became something infinitely more beautiful and lovely, on the border land of which I am now content to stand and gaze. Christ calls us on from higher heights to higher still. It is much to be a son of God, an heir of the heavenly inheritance, but to be such a son as Christ was—One whose doctrine was the Father's truth—One whose sacrifice was the Father's will—One whose inspiration was the Father's love—this is our high calling.

When we wish to make great painters we send them away to the classic halls of Greece and Italy, that they may walk through the galleries and gaze upon the productions of the great masters. We set them down before the famous models, so that, by successive efforts to copy them, they may catch the same lines of grace and drink in something of the same spirit of beauty. But one is our Master, even Christ. Let us look away from ourselves to Him, so that we may catch some rays of the same excellence, that the same spirit may be in us which was also found in Him. We shall come nearer and nearer to Him "till we all with open face beholding as in a glass the glory of the Lord, are changed into the same image from glory to glory, even as by the spirit of the Lord."

HAST THOU FOUND ME, O MINE ENEMY?

"HAST THOU FOUND ME, O MINE ENEMY?"—*1 Kings xxi. 20.*

WHAT a picture we have here of social life in high places! There is the king, the ruler of God's own nation, the successor of David and Solomon, occupying a royal palace, and surrounded with luxury, yet fretting like a petted child because one small garden is not his. In vigorous health, he sickens of a heart disease; with wealth beyond his need, he feels poverty-stricken for lack of a neighbour's plot of ground. There, also, is his wicked queen, like that other queen in tragedy, screwing up the courage of her more feeble consort. Hear her crafty counsel: "Proclaim a fast, and set Naboth on high among the people, and set two men, sons of Belial, before him to bear witness against him, saying, 'Thou didst blaspheme God and the king,' and then carry him out and stone him that he may die." Not daring to go straight at the murderous deed, she must veil her wicked way by name of religion! Simulation of virtue but intensifies the villainy. There, also, are the ready instruments. Like all others in power and position, these royal plotters easily find agents to effect their foul designs. Poor Naboth is publicly confronted, accused, sentenced, stoned, and his possession becomes the king's. Evil is triumphant; but the triumph of evil is its doom. As an old writer has said: "God brings in his bill *at the end* of the meal, not in the middle." Ahab visits the vineyard to gloat over his new acquisition. There he is suddenly confronted by one whom he knew of old—the prophet of God, the fiery Elijah. Ah, how that one stern presence robs the vineyard of its value, and turns its grapes into gall! Behold him cower before that majestic form! Listen to that conscience-stricken exclamation, "Hast thou found me, O mine enemy?" Let us study—

I.—The course and issue of sin.

How fair its semblance when it first allures! It glitters in dazzling garb, obscuring every other object. "Like birds the charming serpent draws," we gaze, and the longer we gaze the more impossible is it to withdraw. All is forgotten—heaven, hell, early lessons, claims of affection, interests of society—everything yields to the Satanic allurement. Viewing the coveted vineyard, reason reels and staggers, conscience becomes stifled, and lawless desire wades through innocent blood to seize its object. For a little while the grapes are luscious, and seem even to cool the fever of passion, but soon the re-action comes, and they become the grapes of Sodom and the clusters of Gomorrah. Reason re-asserts its sway, and proclaims the transgressor a fool. Conscience finds voice to vindicate the victim and vanquish the victor. Heaven frowns on the froward folly; and hell, anticipating its prize, takes possession of the soul.

Take the case of a man selling counterfeit wares, glorying in his sharp practice, gathering where he has not laboured, reaping where he has not sowed. For a while all is well. The glare of success dazzles him. His eyes stand out with fat; he has more than heart can wish. But wait a little. The enemy will find him out—Elijah is even now before him. His ill-gotten gain lies heavy on his hands: it yields him no solid satisfaction. There is more of joy in the mechanics hard-won wage; yea, in "honest poverty" more real wealth than in all the treasures of unscrupulous avarice.

Or, take the sensual man. He enters the domain of vice, cautiously, secretly, with a sense of shame. Gradually, his sensibilities become blunted. Ere long he yields to vices meaner and more grovelling than at first he could have thought of. Every fresh feeling of the heart is hardened, every passion inflamed, and he plunges on in his mad career. Caught by the fatal current, he is hurried along with ever accelerating speed to the swirling maelstrom. Now and then, perhaps, the memory of a departed mother, the kindly advice of an old father, or tender thoughts of his childhood's home flash back upon his soul; but, alas! the bonds of habit are ever strengthening, and he cannot break away. He cannot rise above what he has made himself. See him at last—poor, feeble, and helpless. There he stands like some old volcano — within, hollow, empty, and cold; without, scorched, and wrapped around with the hard lava, which the burning fires had formerly ejected. No glow now, no fire, save that of re-quickened conscience and burning remorse. The end of sin is death.

> "Thus do the dark in soul expire,
> Or live like scorpion girt by fire;
> Thus writhes the mind remorse hath riven,
> Unfit for earth, unmeet for heaven;
> Darkness above, despair beneath,
> Around it flame, within it death."

Let us, then—each and all of us—beware of entrance on any evil course. Avoid the wide, and seek the strait gate. Yesterday, perhaps, some evil temptation assailed you—the opportunity of unrighteous gain or unhallowed indulgence. "Is it not a little one?" you may have said; "May I not yield a little and gain much?" If you yielded, then and there you entered on the road which leadeth to destruction. To-morrow may threaten discovery—may bring the prophet to tell you you have sold yourself to work iniquity. Agitated, alarmed, you may try to bury the wrong in deeper falsehood; but though thus buried, it is not dead, and will not die. The added sin but quickens its vitality and makes it grow. It is a living seed which must needs develop, while other germs of evil gather around, until from that single seed of corruption the soul becomes overgrown with all that is hateful and horrible in habitual lying, knavery, and vice. Long ere such a life comes to a close the soul may have entered hell—the hell of debt, disease, ignominy, and remorse. The evil deed may be done in an instant—in one fleeting, but fatal moment; but conscience never dies; memory never sleeps. Guilt never can become innocence; remorse can never, never whisper peace.

II.—THE ENEMY WILL FIND THEE OUT.

The exclamation of Ahab forcibly illustrates the incontrovertible truth that the wicked man makes an enemy of everything good. Averse to goodness, good must needs be his adversary. "Hast thou found me, O mine enemy?" He calls him his enemy who would fain have been his truest friend. Not one of the sycophants that surrounded his throne had so deep an anxiety for his true welfare. But sin not only blinds the eye—still worse, it perverts the vision. Instead of beholding a friend in Elijah, Ahab's jaundiced eye could see only an enemy. So it frequently is with sin-perverted sight. The faithful monitor becomes the feared and hated foe, the friendly warning is taken for enmity. A bad mind makes every face a mirror in which it beholds, without recognising, its own features. To such the very God of Love Himself presents a stern, repulsive aspect. In Jesus, the friend of sinners, the Jews of old could see only a possessed demoniac, and therefore they crucified Him. And so to the world still the Christ Himself has no beauty that they should desire Him, Christianity seems a system of deceit, its ministers are hateful, and every believer is regarded as a hypocrite.

Of this projected and refracted enmity there are numberless illustrations. Joseph, the amiable and beautiful, was hated by his brethren, and therefore deemed their enemy. David, the most loyal and faithful servant of Saul, was by Saul regarded as a scheming usurper waiting to vault into his throne. The evil he saw in the youth existed only in his own wild, ugly passion; yet, instead of strangling that, as he should, he tried to murder David. So also with another Saul—afterwards named Paul. The Jews of his day, when he sought to win them back to the Messiah they had rejected, could see in him only the renegade which they themselves really were, and thus they compassed heaven and earth to work his destruction.

And so also in the present. The passionate, ill-natured man is an example, living always in stormy weather, even while spring and summer smile around him — always wronged, always hurt, always complaining of some enemy. He has no conception that this enemy is in his own bosom —in the sourness, the ungoverned irritability, the habitual reflection of his own bad spirit and character. Let him exorcise these hateful demons, and he will find the enemies of his delusion friends worthy of his confidence.

"The same is true of the fretful—those who wear away fast and die because they have worried life out. With them everything is wrong, and no one ever does right. Husband, wife, child, friend, customer, and minister—all are wrong. They are pricked and stung at every turn and nothing frets them more than to see others get along so smoothly. To them life is a field of nettles, just because of their own stinging tempers. Would they but cast these aside, they might tread on cloth of gold and sleep on beds of down. But, the truth is, most of us are too apt to fall into this mood—to imagine some fault in our condition or surroundings. We wonder why God has given such a desert to live in, never dreaming that the desert is not around, but within us—an immense Sahara, wider and more dreary than Africa knows."

A bad temper, a wrong love, ungoverned pride, restless ambition, corrupt principle—these are the real thorns of life. Oh! that men could be so far disenchanted as to see that their condition is what they themselves are; and that it can be only bad, and ever bad, so long as they are bad, even were all the wealth, power, and splendour of the world laid at their feet.

And it is well it should be so. Thus evil checks and chides itself, hinting all the while at the needed remedy. At enmity with God, we meet not only His servants and messages, but even His blessings with antagonism. To all the exclamation of the carnal heart is, "Hast thou found me, O mine enemy?"

But into our own sin-blighted world One has come to destroy the enmity. Jesus has come as the Great Physician to cure those diseased souls of ours, to correct our perverted vision, and enable us to see things as they really are. "In His light ye shall see light." In Him is life, and the life is the light of men. The darkness shall flee away; all obscurity, all misunderstanding shall be removed. It will be a new world to you. Nothing in the providence or in the world of God shall seem wrong or out of place. No cause of grumbling, no need to fret. Brother to brother shall be true; neighbour with neighbour shall see eye to eye. The heart put right, nothing outside of it shall be wrong; and never, never more shall conscience wring from your soul the agonising exclamation, "Hast thou found me, O mine enemy?" Nay, in Him ye shall find a friend who sticketh closer than a brother — One who will make you His brother and give you His nature. Thus renewed within, and living in the pure element of His love, this world shall become a realm of beauty, a paradise of peace, a feast of satisfying good, an instrument of joyous harmony; while the eye of faith, with unwavering confidence, shall look forward to a brighter land beyond, where no enemy can ever enter to mar your happiness, or disturb the universal and eternal peace.

WORK OUT YOUR OWN SALVATION.

"WORK OUT YOUR OWN SALVATION WITH FEAR AND TREMBLING FOR IT IS GOD WHICH WORKETH IN YOU, BOTH TO WILL AND TO DO OF HIS GOOD PLEASURE.—*Phil. ii. 12, 13.*

(*Preached in St. Andrew's, Victoria, 1870.*)

THIS passage affirms the union of the Divine and human agencies in the work of salvation, and varied are the difficulties which have been gathered around it. Controversial theology has found in this a favourite field; and many, tired of controversy, have found expression of their belief on this point in the words of Dr. Johnson, when questioned on the doctrine of necessity—"All theory is for it; all experience against it; we reason that we are bound by necessity; we feel that we are free."

The subject has not only severed friends, but rent churches asunder. Wesley and Whitfield, after many years of peaceful intercourse, differed so much about it that they preached publicly against each other, and divided their followers into the two branches of Calvinistic and Wesleyan Methodists. In 1618 the Synod of Holland met in Dort for the final determination of this doctrine. It occupied their deliberations for months, and when Arminius and his disciples were excommunicated, it almost led to a civil war. In Scotland it has led to various schisms, and received more importance than it really deserves. Instead of receiving both—God's sovereignty and man's free agency—as they are presented together in His Word, different parties have seized upon one or the other and placed them in opposition; the one wresting God's sceptre from His hand, lest man should seem a slave; the other binding man with an iron fetter, lest God should not seem a sovereign; and thus the strength of Christian thought has been wasted. God presents them both as truths, and as harmonious truths, both being part of the one great unity of truth; but man, unsatisfied, seeks to reconcile them in his own mind, steering away from the plain paths into the dizzy heights of profitless speculation, and there flutters

> "Like adventurous bird, that hath outflown
> Its strength upon the sea—ambition wrecked—
> A thing the thrush might pity as she sits
> Brooding in quiet upon her lowly nest."

Now, this passage is not given by the Apostle as the basis of controversy, but as an encouragement to work. "Work," says the Apostle, "for it is God which worketh in you."

We find analogies to this in nature. Man is a worker in other fields, just because God's laws bind him and all things around him. Without God he cannot turn himself to any good work. Because God's winds blow, he spreads his canvas to the breeze. Because God's planets revolve in undeviating constancy, he sows in spring and reaps in autumn. Take a case in mechanics, as perhaps the most simple. A man sets himself to the construction of a ship or a house. He first conceives its plan or form. The mind which conceives it is a ray of the Eternal; the faculties of imagination, abstraction, memory, and judgment are all derivations from the Supreme Intelligence. In gathering his materials, he again draws from the stores of the Almighty. All through the ages God has been preparing these. Fire and flood have burst forth to melt and mould them. He thus reaps the result of agencies at work long before he came into conscious existence. In transporting the materials he takes advantage of the winds and waves that are the swift messengers of the Almighty. He raises them to their places by machines that do not create power, but merely transmit and direct it. In all this he is aided by laws, of which he knows little more than that they serve his purpose. Trusting himself to God's laws, he yet acts freely. He works, yet God meets him at every turn. He builds, yet it is God which buildeth in him. The great act of creation is so far renewed through the instrumentality of man made in the image of God. In like manner the disciple, in loving and trusting and doing good, is bound by moral laws and aided by them, as the builder is bound by laws in mechanics and aided by them. The influences which regenerate human nature and renew our earth-bound souls are of God. It is God working in us to will and to do. It is working just because God has given us power to work, the materials to work with, the motives to work, the laws by which we work; nay, the very joy of our work is part of the joy of God. We perceive God's agencies everywhere, as well as in the soul of man. We readily acknowledge these agencies of God in perfecting the produce of the field, which to-day is and to-morrow passes away; and how much more is such agency required to unfold and educate the moral life which never dies. We may call it in the one case a process of nature; in the other, an operation of the Spirit. "There are diversities of operations; but it is the same God that worketh all in all."

We have seen in an orrery one motion carrying all the parts around a central sun, whilst within there were many separate motions. Here the globe, representing the earth, moving in one direction; there is Jupiter, revolving from north to south, and his satellites in a different direction. We behold Saturn and his eight satellites, Uranus and his six. The system sweeps around, whilst within are other smaller systems moving in contrary directions, in transverse directions, in parallel directions, yet all obedient to one moving spring. This is simply an illustration, but it may aid us in the conception of the one great will controlling all; whilst within are the myriad thousand lesser wills, some acting in loving sympathy, some in fancied opposition, all willing and doing, yet God working in them to will and to do.

II.—WORK OUT YOUR OWN SALVATION.

Many suppose that liberty consists in doing what we please. This is a mistake. There may be the utmost liberty in doing what we ought rather than what we please. True liberty consists in our full sympathy with God and His plans; the perception that God's purpose is a righteous purpose, and that it embraces our own good. Then we act, not as blind instruments, but as joyous fellow-workers. Our wills being in harmony with His will, "we walk at liberty seeking His precepts." His spirit being within us, we "work it out" in the common rounds of life. A demand is thus made for work. Though we are not saved for our work, yet we are saved according to our work. Salvation is not mere deliverance from the punishment of sin; it is deliverance from sin itself. It is an easy thing to feel a sentimental sadness over past errors; it is easy to utter eloquent prayers, to sing joyous hallelujahs, and to imagine ourselves very happy. But to bear our burden, to carry our cross, to persevere in a life of self-denial, of prayer, of obedience—this is a hard thing. It is a work, it is a battle, it is a race.

Work out your own salvation.—There is a strong emphasis

here on the words "*your own.*" There is something to be done which no one can do for you. No beloved friend can save you, no teaching minister, no praying Christian, no guardian angel, not even God Himself, save as you fall in with His gracious operations. This is your own work. Not something you are to pray God to do for you, but to do for yourselves. God's work is already done. God's love in Jesus Christ has been declared. God's Spirit hath come. Turn ye then to "your work"—"your own salvation." The wearer of the crown must be the winner of the crown. Look at Paul. His theory of religion was not that of a glad voyage over tranquil waters. To him it was a work. It was the great inspiration of his life, passing beyond sanctuaries and Sabbaths into the whole economy of the secular and social. The gospel he preached was a gospel he practised. The cross he gloried in was a cross he carried. Paul made tents in the workshop of Aquila; but "Holiness to the Lord" was inscribed on the tent shop. "These are Christ's" was written on every tool of his bench, and on the cord, and on the canvas. Amidst all his unwearying toil for others, his most earnest care was "to keep his own body under," that he himself should not at last be a castaway. Before his faith-lit eye, was ever flashing at life's far goal heaven's unfading crown; and, like the Grecian athlete, night and day, might and main, body and soul, he strove and struggled for it. And spite of all our notions, there is no other way—no easier way than Paul's for our own progress. Yet how little are we like him! Alas! my brethren, if we toiled as listlessly for this world as for heaven, the merchant would become bankrupt, and the artizan a beggar by the wayside. A child, weaving for himself a chaplet of flowers, toils in their gathering more earnestly than we in setting stars in our crown of rejoicing.

The high calling of God in Christ Jesus is not to passive indolence, but to earnest work. Behold the imperilled mariner! How he rouses himself in mighty energy, with rudder and sail, to escape for his life. What tremendous efforts men put forth when the precipice is crumbling under their feet, or the earthquake rocking their dwellings! How then ought they to labour when "working out their own salvation!"

III.—WITH FEAR AND TREMBLING.

There is a slavish fear of God which paralyses effort. We may be sure that Paul did not mean that. He knew in whom he had believed. He had experienced the ceaseless loving-kindness of the Father. He leaned himself on the Rock and Refuge of weary souls. He would not have Christians to be terror-stricken, but to be impressed with that anxiety and concern correspondent to the importance of the work—with a joyous sense of what God has done for them, to spring forward to the conflict.

With fear and trembling.—For great are the gifts we use. If the spirit which inclines us to God is a derivation from the Most High, if the means we employ are God's, if the laws that accelerate spiritual growth are really God's, how careful should we be in the use of them: how fearful lest they be misapplied!

The man that carries rich treasures upon some dark and difficult path, walks with fear and trembling; so ought we with such a treasure as our soul, and in the use of instrumentalities that might quicken the brightest angel around the throne on high.

With fear and trembling.—Great interests are at stake. It is working out not merely our comfort or our prosperity, but salvation—our own salvation—the salvation of our immortal soul. Our salvation may be of little importance to the world, but to us it is of more importance than all the world. There is a sad tendency to be at ease in Zion, to leave the whole earnest work of salvation to God, to act, and speak, and think as the world does. There is need of Christian separateness; the enduring of hardness, the running with patience. A firm believer was Paul in the doctrine that salvation is all of grace, yet it had no tendency in his mind to lull into security. To the very end of his life we find him, with all his intensest energies, stemming the flood and fighting the battle, lest he himself should be a castaway. If God bend down from His throne to strengthen us, how fearful must the battle be! Easier is it to carry by storm a hundred walled cities than to conquer ourselves. What need then of fear and trembling!

With fear and trembling.—For the very laws of God, which aid us when we do work, are against us when we do not work. The philosopher who first thought of conducting the lightning from the skies, though sure of the law, applied himself to the first experiment with fear and trembling. As he thought of the greatness of the agent with which he was dealing, and its mighty power to help or hurt, his heart throbbed and his hand became tremulous. And shall we, who venture ourselves upon the spiritual laws of God's universe, not walk with fear and trembling? Shall we who are dealing with instrumentalities mightier far and more delicate, not tremble under a sense of our responsibility?

Work!—Whatever men may say of the will of God, that is the will of God for you.

Work!—God Almighty calls you to be fellow-workers with Him, though humble be your sphere of duty.

Work!—That is the best cure for abstract difficulties and cankering affections.

With fear and trembling.—The fragments of ten thousand wrecks, that bestrew the whole shore of time, proclaim the importance of *your own* salvation.

With fear and trembling.—For you bear within you an image that may be brightened with the glory of heaven, or soiled past all hope of cleansing.

With fear and trembling.—For those very laws, which, if used, will bear you up to God's own home, abused, will break in fearful judgment against you.

BE STRONG: QUIT YOU LIKE MEN!

"BE STRONG: QUIT YOU LIKE MEN!"—*1 Cor. xvi. 13.*
(Preached to Volunteers of Victoria, June, 1867.)

I. "BE strong!" Strength, in some form or other, is the chief quality of life. It is that which all respect. In the earlier stages of civilization we find the enthronement of mere physical strength. Among the Greeks it was deified in Jove. The Supreme was he who could terrify gods and men by his mighty hand, and launch forth thunderbolts upon his enemies. There was little recognition of higher strength—of moral power. They even ascribed to him cruelty and licentiousness, on the principle that one so mighty might do as he pleased. Among the old Romans, too, virtue was valour. It was for the military hero they created their triumphal arches, prepared their laurel crowns, and called for the poet's lays. It was the same, too, among our own early ancestors. The king of men was the physically strong man. Our very word "king" comes from this. According to the original signification, it is the man who can do most—the canning man—the king man. They all worshipped mere physical strength. They did not realize that he who ruleth his spirit is better than he who taketh a city—that a greater victory may be gained in the silent chambers of the soul than amid the din and pomp of a battlefield. But Christianity has placed us on a higher platform. Our Lord was physically a weak man. When His disciples, after a journey, were able to go and buy bread, He sat wearied by the wayside well. But he was spiritually strong. This Paul, who says, "Be strong: quit you like men!" was physically weak—small of stature, partially lame, partially blind; he was in soul one of the strongest men. Christianity has taught us to see more strength in a young man struggling with the difficulties of his position than in a Hercules strangling monsters—to see more strength in a weak woman clinging to great and noble purposes, amid burdens heavy to be borne, than in Alexander conquering the world—to see more strength in a sick girl submitting to her lot amid penury and neglect, than in the great military emperor who kept Europe ablaze for half-a-century, and pined like a petted child in his imprisonment. Christianity has taught us that virtue is valour, but not in the old Roman sense. It is strength of will, not of arm; moral power, not brute force; true principle, not passages-at-arms.

> For what is strength? Without a double share of wisdom,
> Vast, unwieldy, burdensome;
> Proudly secure, yet liable to fall
> By weakest subtleties; strength's not made to rule,
> But to subserve where wisdom bears command.

"Be strong: quit you like men!" A great theological writer—Müller, in his book on the doctrine of sin—has stated that sin is not a real thing in the universe—that it is rather the absence of a real thing—the lack of controlling power, of moral strength. That it is like cold, which is not a real thing, but the absence of caloric—the heat principle. This is a suggestive thought—that all sin is, in fact, weakness. The world was made by God all good. Everything in it is intended by Him for good, and sin enters because men have not moral strength to apply the things of the world to their destined purposes; and it is lamentable to think that every vice is the perversion of some virtue—that every evil is the distortion of designed good—that the worst passions that ever hurried a poor wretch to destruction are the lawless, unrestrained abuse of faculties and feelings that might have been trained for heaven. Man's nature consists of two parts: there are the springs of action and the guides of action. The springs of action are instinct, appetite, passion, disposition, habit; and they are all necessary and helpful in their place. These ever urge on to action. But there are the guides of action : conscience and reason. These are to direct and control. The evil is that the subordinate powers are ever apt to assume the mastery. Then is man like a chariot dragged downhill by the fiery steeds, without guard or driver: command is lost, and wreck is imminent.

Thus the very powers that lift a man upward, if controlled, become instruments of speedy destruction, if uncontrolled. Many a man, instead of conquering the world, lets the world conquer him. Instead of possessing the world, he lets the world possess him. Sad it is for a man thus to fall before the world; and yet how many do we see every day who have yielded to the world without even a struggle—spirits made only a little lower than the angels falling lower than the brute—immortal souls soaked into the flesh and sharing the rottenness of the bones ! If you should find some statue of beautiful proportions and wondrous inspiration cast from its pedestal—lying upon its face—shattered, disfigured, and soiled in the mire, you would mourn over the desecration. You would say, What lost wealth ! What wasted labour ! Into this block of marble genius wrought its energies and breathed its living soul, and now it lies there thrown down and trampled upon. But what is the statue to the living man that has fallen from his high position? God wrought within that man His own image. He breathed into that man His own nature. He sent him into the world not to be as a mere statue, a dull and motionless shape, but to be a growing and exhaustless force. The world was spread out before him to be seized and conquered. Realms of infinite truth and beauty burst open before him. Springs of true enjoyment opened out around him—elements of power— the possibilities that await every soul born into the world crowded on his right hand and his left. But the world challenged him through his appetites, and he went down before them. They defaced his image; they have torn off his crown. They have beaten and trampled him into the brutal mass which you see before you.

But this is only one mode of attack. There are thousands who are not the victims of vice, and yet the world has possession of their hearts. It pleads with their vanity. It provokes the lust of fame. It plots in the schemes of the mart, in the lists of ambition, in the circle of fashion. Therefore saith the Apostle: "Watch ye: stand fast in the faith." Watch ye! for your enemies are many, and subtle as they are strong, and more to be dreaded in their secret whispers to the soul than in their grosser forms of evil. Watch ye! for you wrestle not against enemies of flesh and blood, but against principalities and powers, against the rulers of the darkness of this world, and spiritual wickedness in high places. "Stand fast in the faith!" Look up to Him who has promised heavenly strength. Take to you the helmet of salvation and the sword of the Spirit, that ye may be able to stand in the evil day.

II. "Like men!" A holy Exemplar has been given. Once only has there been set before the world the perfect man. The Son of God became the Son of Man. In Him we see what life should be. He shows us what we might be if true, and what we are not, because untrue. In Him we behold unbroken strength and ineffable tenderness marvellously combined. The temptations brought to bear upon Him were as powerless as the feathered darts against the shining shield. Altogether righteous, He could yet protect the erring woman from the mercilessness of her accusers. Ever brave in meeting opposition and wrong, he could yet feel for the disciple who, faithless, had gone astray. Though not intimidated before kings and mighty men, yet a little child could ever move His heart. In Him was life divinely human and altogether beautiful. He could calmly say: "I, if I be lifted up, will draw all men unto Me." That life has been lifted up in our world, and it has drawn men up out of their brutality and selfishness into gentleness and sacrifice. HUMANITY has had a different meaning ever since Christ lived among men. No wonder that the Apostle in urging the truly heroic life, says, "Looking unto Jesus, the author and finisher of our faith; who for the joy that was set before Him, endured the cross, despising the shame, and is set down at the right hand of the throne of God. For consider Him that endured such contradiction of sinners against Himself, lest ye be wearied and faint in your minds. Ye have not yet resisted unto blood, striving against sin."

And if we have striven and been overcome, if we have fallen in the battle of life and lie wounded by the wayside, to whom can we look but unto Him. In Him there is pardon for the past and strength for the future. "The bruised reed He will not break, the smoking flax he will not quench." In His Divine compassion He will turn to us, all unworthy as we are, and say, "Rise, walk! Jesus of Nazareth biddeth thee." "Be strong: quit ye like men!"

"Quit you like men!" I like that phrase. Many are the famous battle calls—none better than this. It falls short and sharp from the Apostle who fought a good fight and obtained an eternal crown.

"Quit you like men!" How suggestive the phrase—like men!

> I dare do all that becomes a man.
> He who dares do more is none.

"Quit you like men!" Like men for whom the Lord died. He took not upon Him the nature of angels, but of men.

"Quit you like men!" Men whose days are as an handbreadth—whose age is as nothing before Him. Your life is even as a vapour that appeareth for a little and then vanisheth away. The day approaches that fixes your fate for ever—the hours even now are passing which bear along with them your eternal happiness or eternal misery.

In that sad civil war between the Northern and Southern States of America, the army of the North under Grant seemed to make but little progress. More than once members of the Cabinet remonstrated with him and advised him to change his tactics. At length the General, in one of those short sentences that have the ring of true eloquence, wrote in reply to the Minister of War: "I propose to fight it out on this line though it take me all the summer." And so we, planting ourselves under the banner of our Lord and Saviour Jesus Christ—with freedom, victory, heaven, and immortality all in view—reply to all who seek to seduce us: "We will fight it out on this line though it take us all our lives."

MY SOUL CLEAVETH TO THE DUST.

"MY SOUL CLEAVETH TO THE DUST: BUT QUICKEN THOU ME ACCORDING TO THY WORD.—*Psalm cxix. 25.*

(*Last Sermon in Old College Church, October, 1876.*)

AN old writer has well said, "The book of Psalms is placed in the heart of the Bible, for it reveals the heart of all humanity." God poured streams of feeling into David's heart and brought marvellous skill of music to his right hand. Carefully was he educated by God for giving to His Church a perpetual liturgy and litany. He led him the round of all human conditions, that he might catch the spirit proper to each, and utter it according to truth. He brought him up amid the sheep pastures, that the groundwork of his character might be laid among the simple and universal forms of feeling. He placed him in the palace, that he might have ideas of majesty and power, of nobleness and glory. He carried him to the solitudes of the wilderness, that his soul might form the sublime conceptions of God and of His great works. He made him an exile and an outlaw, that he might depend on the providence of God. His trials were but the tuning of the instrument with which the spirit might express the many voices of the earth. As some skilled musician upon the strings of his harp, he touches the different chords of the heart, and evokes from each its separate utterance. Every feeling, whether of joy or sorrow, of fear or of hope, of penitence or of faith, is there expressed in its intensest form. Even by his backslidings David became better able to utter forth every form of spiritual experience.

This Psalm is in praise of the law of God. He contemplates the glory of God as revealed in His holy and good law. He speaks of God's righteous judgments, of God's testimonies, of God's word. As the painter gazes upon some famous masterpiece in every light, and contemplates it from every point of view, so the shepherd king surveys the law of God in all its different aspects. But just as the man who stands before some clear and brilliant light discovers the dust upon his raiment, so, gazing upon this clear law of God, his own departure from it stands out to view. In almost every verse the contrast is maintained between the purity of God's law and his own weakness. "Incline my heart unto Thy testimonies, and not to covetousness." "Thy word have I hid in mine heart, that I might not sin against Thee." "Blessed art Thou, O Lord: teach me Thy statutes." It appears as if at this point (verse 25) he had paused in meditation upon his past life; and reflecting how often the council had been despised, how often his vows had been broken, how often his soul had been steeped in sense and sin, resumed again his song in penitential strain: "My soul cleaveth to the dust: but quicken Thou me according to Thy word."

I.—"MY SOUL CLEAVETH TO THE DUST."

True, O David, king of Israel! God's anointed though thou wert, yet sadly didst thou stain thy regal dignity. Dost thou remember that letter sent to Joab by the hand of Uriah? or that time when Nathan, the prophet of God, stood before thee? or that night when thou wert crying in the gate, whilst the sick child of thy transgression was dying within the palace walls? Oh, thine offence, how rank it rose to heaven! Let us, however, remember that if David was a man of strong passions, if he soiled his royal dignity, if he did what was mean and sensual and base, there is a whole-heartedness about his confession of sin. If his guilt was black, his repentance was bitter. Of all who have sinned as David sinned, few have repented as David repented. We see him lying low in the dust; but we hear also his earnest cry ascending heavenward: "Have mercy upon me, O God, according to Thy loving kindness!" Mark the depth of this expression: "My soul cleaveth to the dust." Here are two things brought together, which are utterly contrary in their nature—soul and dust. The soul, the breath of the Almighty, a ray from the Infinite Himself, immortal in its destiny, noble in all the expansion of its powers, and heavenly in its aspirations—this is brought into contact with dust, that which is earthly, perishable, dead, unclean. And not the dust as we understand it—not the soft, fresh soil into which the seed is cast and nourished until it sendeth forth the bud and the tender blade, but, as the original signifies, the hard, dry, beaten pavement—that which is barren, unclean, and trodden under foot of men. What a depth of degradation! The soul clinging to the dust! We have seen the delicate cirrus cloud, born of the breeze in the serenest sky, rolling around the hard, dry lava on the mountain summit; we have seen the beautiful sunlight resting on the foul and pestilential den; we have seen the flowers of beauty cast around the cold clay corpse; we have seen the chambers of a once famous temple filled with all loathsome things; but saddest of all pictures is that of the soul cleaving to the inharmonious dust—the spiritual subordinated to the material—the incorruptible merging itself with the corruptible. Yet sad as the picture is, it is one which is often seen. The man in our Saviour's parable congratulated his soul by saying, "Soul, thou hast much goods laid up for many years." He, like many others, brought goods to the soul—the material to the spiritual. But the soul will not be at ease with these. With aspirations which reach the heavens, it is restless when confined to anything lower. Created immortal, nothing that is merely material can ever satisfy it. Ah! my brethren, what a strange thing is this heart of man! In itself no larger than a bird of the air, and yet the whole world will not fill it. Restless, the cry will ever arise, "Give, give." Its capacity partakes of the infinitude of Him who made it; and it never rests until God Himself enters and enthrones Himself upon all its powers. Then there is light, conviction, and knowledge; then there is harmony, and fulness, and peace. The heart of man, like a wearied child, has repose alone on the bosom of the Father.

"My soul cleaveth to the dust." It is not mere accidental contact, occasional transgression, which the Psalmist mourns over, but a lingering degradation of nature, in spite of effort and prayer. "My soul *cleaveth* to the dust." In that one word we find the condensed history of a protracted warfare between the spiritual and the carnal. In reviewing his life, he upbraids the traitorous soul which had so often made alliance with the enemy. At times she had mounted on the wings of fervent faith and burning desire, and carried him to the very gate of heaven in sweet communion; at other times, drooped her ethereal pinions, and trailed her powers upon the ground. Often had she dwelt with fulness of joy in the presence of God; but alas! again and again fallen back upon the earth and the dust.

As our eye rests upon this expression, there come up to memory the fervent aspirations of his youth nurtured on the plains of Bethlehem; his bold defiance of his country's enemy in the name of God; his magnanimity towards Saul when his life was in his hand; his generous friendship for Jonathan; his princely kindness to the helpless Mephibosheth; his eager desire that the Ark of God should find a resting-place; those spiritual songs that showed how he walked with God and talked with God. But what are these that also present themselves? Rash outbursts of passion, acts of violence and of vileness, deeds of selfishness and sensuality, the soul fluttering and falling to the dust—cleaving to the dust, for the very sunset of his life is darkened. What a struggle of purity with passion, of light with darkness, his life reveals! How lamentable that he who said, "As the hart panteth after the water-brooks, so panteth my soul after God," should so soon after be compelled to utter the melancholy wail: "Behold I was shapen in iniquity, and in sin did my mother conceive me!"

"My soul cleaveth to the dust." Do not these words come home to you this morning? Has not your life been a spiritual struggle—confession of sin, and yet cleaving to sin? Good resolutions at the table of the Lord, and small performance in the paths of life. "The heart knoweth its own bitterness." There are three lives which all of us lead:—There is the life by which we are known to the world—our public character; there is the life by which we are known to our family circle—our domestic character; and there is that other life within the precincts of our own hearts. We have these three lives, not because we are intentionally hypocritical, but because the different conditions of each develop into different manifestations. Many will be inclined to say that the public character is the best, the domestic next best, and the secret life the worst. This is not my opinion. I believe that the secret life, that life of thought and aspiration within our soul, is the best. I am certain that could we penetrate through the drapery which hides each soul, we would find many a bright ideal fondly cherished, many longings after the things that are lovely and pure, and many vows and efforts of the soul to redeem her fading majesty. I believe that if all were known, many, very many, are better than the world takes them to be. But just as our unknown aspirations are the highest, so also are our hidden sins the blackest. Each man knoweth his own sore and his own sickness. Each man beareth his own burden—a heavy burden that is to some of us. It may be that some one has a burden, the very name of which would cause him to start in alarm. There is that foul deed that lies as a load upon the heart; the memory of that one whose hopes were utterly blasted by our perversity; that act of meanness that makes us at times despise ourselves; that crime, it may be, which might have blasted our fair reputation. One may have some besetting sin that has caused him to fall again and again—a serpent which he has nursed in his bosom for years; some enemy that enters by the door of appetite, or of passion, or of temper, or of habit; some darling vice against which he has fought and struggled and prayed. My friend, is there ever a thought crosses your mind which makes you instinctively cry to Heaven for mercy? Is it not yours to say with the Psalmist, as these bitter memories come up, "My soul cleaveth to the dust"?

II.—Mark not only the confession, but the prayer:

"Quicken Thou me."

The spiritual and the material are in every man. God created us in His own image; and just as we have seen the artist developing, bringing out into view the picture which the sun's rays have depicted upon his plate, so may the image of God within man, which has been soiled and stained by sin, be again renewed and quickened by the Spirit of God. "We all, with open face, beholding as in a glass the glory of the Lord, are changed into the same image, from glory to glory, even as by the Spirit of the Lord." Conscience and reason are the spiritual parts of our nature, and we are restored to the image of God in so far as they bear supreme sway. The evil is, that the parts of our nature intended to be subordinate so often usurp the place of these. We too often act from impulse, or instinct, or appetite, or bad habit. As we have seen the rich soil of a neglected garden spend itself in luxuriant, though noxious herbage, so too often the whole nature runs into selfishness and sensuality; the diviner parts are overlapped and hidden. Our Saviour, referring to this, said: "The kingdom of God is like unto a treasure *buried* in a field." The flowers bloom there, and the long grass waves there, and as men pass by they say it is beautiful, forgetful that this very beauty, this luxuriant growth, in reality conceals the treasure. Thus is it in our life. Worldly pursuits, sensuous charms, external possessions attract the eyes and command the highest efforts, whilst that priceless treasure, the soul, is lost sight of. We all feel this. Well then may we cry, "Quicken Thou me." There is in every man a germ of goodness, which may be quickened by the Spirit of God into strong and hardy life. Who is here so poor in thought and affection as not to feel this? Who is so utterly degraded as not sometimes to be touched by the beauty of holiness? Who is so thoroughly bad as not sometimes to respond, through every chord of his being, to the call of virtue, generosity, and honour? Who is there with soul so dead as not sometimes to be touched by the nobleness of affection and self-sacrifice? Who has not at times felt the love of Christ which passeth knowledge?

Who has not at times experienced the ecstasy of spiritual strength—a foretaste of the joy unspeakable and full of glory? Such experiences tell us that we have not yet come up to our fullest capacity. Even amid the dust of the earth we have had occasional glimpses of the realms of undiscovered moral beauty that lie within each one of us— realms which, like the cities buried of old, may yet be revealed in the clear light of heaven. And what should a man care for so much as this—the strengthening of the Divine life within his soul? What office, what apparel, what worldly honour is there worthy of comparison with the soul which a man bears within him? What circumstances of outward grandeur can lend such dignity as the throne of inward light and being where the spirit lives for ever? What object can possibly be set before us so worthy of effort, and agony, and prayer as the quickening of the soul to all that is pure, good, beautiful. It was for this that Jesus loved us and gave Himself for us. He saw us not only as we are, but as what, through His Spirit, we might be. No longer prone in the dust, no longer steeped in sense and sin, but standing erect and firm, our face toward heaven, and our soul radiant with holy beauty; and thus He spoke to us: "My brothers, children of a common Father, the power of endless being still is yours; the possibility of eternal progress still is yours. The Spirit of God still is yours. Rise! Walk!" In view of all that He has done, and of all that He will do, well may the prayer rise from each heart: "Quicken Thou me!"

III.—"According to Thy Word."

The Psalmist, in his struggle for a diviner life, falls back upon God's Word. In the same psalm he says: "I hope in Thy Word;" "I trust in Thy Word;" "I will not forget Thy Word." Feeling his own helplessness, he falls back upon God's promised helpfulness. He speaks from his personal experience—"Thy Word hath quickened me." This is as true to us as to him. The Word is the instrument of the Spirit. The Saviour himself defied the Tempter with the Word of God. The Apostle says that "the Word of God is quick and powerful, and sharper than any two-edged sword, piercing even to the dividing asunder of soul and spirit, and joints and marrow, and is a discerner of the thoughts and intents of the heart." Let this Word, then, be the weapon of our warfare. Use it freely, and the Spirit will quicken it for the good of our souls. It will warn us of many a danger. Its bright promises will win us to many an effort. Its holy precepts will guide us in many a difficult path. "Let the word of Christ dwell in you richly in all wisdom." Like David, let us plead the Word before the throne. And surely, when we remember how often we have confessed our Lord with our lips, and yet denied Him by our lives; how often we have sat at His table, and yet served His enemies; how often we cried for mercy, and yet cleaved to the dust—this prayer of old will come home to our hearts to-day: "My soul cleaveth to the dust; but quicken Thou me, according to Thy Word."

> In the hour of my distresse,
> When temptations me oppresse,
> And when I my sins confesse,
>   Sweet Spirit, comfort me!
>
> When I lie within my bed,
> Sick in heart and sore in head,
> And with doubts disquieted,
>   Sweet Spirit, comfort me!
>
> When the passing bell doth tolle,
> And the furies, in a shoal,
> Come to fright my parting soul,
>   Sweet Spirit, comfort me!

GROW IN GRACE.

"GROW IN GRACE, AND IN THE KNOWLEDGE OF OUR LORD AND SAVIOUR JESUS CHRIST."—*2 Peter iii. 18.*

(*Preached on the Opening of Blackfriars, 14th October, 1877.*)

IN the vegetable kingdom we find first the blade, and then the ear, and then the full corn in the ear. So also in the animal kingdom, the periods of infancy and feebleness are gradually followed by those of strength and maturity; and the higher in the scale of being, the longer in the reaching of ripeness. In man there is a greater distance between his birth-point and his perfection than in any of the other creatures. He is longer in coming into possession of even his physical faculties. The lamb dropped of a morning upon the lea skips at evening more nimbly than its dam; but the conqueror of the world is born an infant, scarce able to turn itself. He has to creep and stumble, and touch and handle for many a day, ere able to take his place with those around him. In his intellectual life this is even more the case. He has to add line upon line, precept upon precept, gather here a little and there a little before he reaps the treasures of wisdom and knowledge. But here man, while still exemplifying the law of gradual growth, starts off from all other creatures, in the fact that he has no period of ripeness. There never was a man that drunk dry the cup of knowledge. Beyond the most far-seeing of our race there stretched territories they never saw. Above the giants of our humanity there rose heights they never climbed. Like the camp-fires we used to kindle in the forest, the widening circle of their light revealed the ever-widening circles of the darkness around. But it is in regard to man's spiritual nature that we behold most markedly the immeasurable distance between the initial stage and the final development. The law of his soul is life—life, ever growing, more abundant, and glorious. Even the material things amid which he is placed to toil and struggle suggest the immense possibilities of his existence. The things that are seen bring to view the unseen; the finite bears him up to the infinite; and time carries his thoughts forward into eternity. As with a telescope, a few feet in length, man learns to survey the heavens above him, worlds beyond worlds, so even now, with the aid of his limited faculties, does he rise to the conception of what is beyond the visible world, beyond all conceivable time, beyond all imagined power and beauty and glory. Confined as the spirit is within the narrow compass of the body, yet there stream out from it the rays of thought to infinity, to eternity, to boundless grandeur and goodness. Around and beyond the spirit's eye there lie outstretched the infinite and everlasting paths. What a splendid field, then, for the loftiest ambition, for the purest aspiration, is thus brought before us by the injunction of the Apostle: "Grow in grace, and in the knowledge of our Lord and Saviour Jesus Christ."

I.—Grow in Grace.

To the ancient Greek the beautiful was identified with the good. The same term stood for both. The New Testament also identifies grace and goodness. But it has lifted up the word into a sense the Grecian never knew. The

Apostles say little about beauty or grace in outward form, but they speak much of grace or beauty in moral qualities. The spiritual man in their eye had not only good qualities, but good qualities in balance and harmony and sweetness— not only moral excellence, but moral shapeliness and symmetry. He was to be pre-eminently the man of grace. The moral nature, in the image of God, is the most beautiful thing upon earth. God never made anything so beautiful as He made man to be. There is no picture that was ever painted, there is no statue that was ever carved, there is no work of art ever conceived that was ever half so beautiful as a living man renewed in the image of the Lord Jesus Christ. The most beautiful temple cannot for a moment be compared to the soul that seeks its shrine in the love of God and in the love of man. The richest music that will ever be struck by the hand of man from instruments can never equal in power and sweetness the music of the purified heart. No voice ever lifted up in pulpit can equal in attractiveness the ministry of warm affection and of faithful sacrifice. To thus grow in grace is the chief end of men. It is not what we make in business, but what the business makes of us, which is the great question. The inward result, not the outward estate, ought to be the supreme interest Alas! that we should so often find the sad contrast between what ought to be and what is. Offices and stocks and mercantile privileges are the ruling interests, not growth of the soul. Currency has value, and bonds have value, and broad lands, and freighted ships, and rich mines are all marked down in strict account; but the storied treasures of the heart, the unfathomable mines that are to be wrought in the soul, the broad and boundless realms of thought, the freighted ocean of man's affection, of his love, of his faith, of his hope—who regards these? Who seeks for them as if they were brighter than gold and dearer than treasure?

II.—The Knowledge of the Lord Jesus Christ.

It need scarcely be said that the Apostle has been warning the disciples of false teachers and their doctrines, and that a contrast is here implied between the knowledge of the Lord Jesus Christ and the Gnosis of the period that has preceded and was even then influencing the minds of men. And we do well to remember always what the world was, without the knowledge of the Lord Jesus Christ. It seems as if it had been the purpose of God to let man do all that man could do to discover truth of himself. A succession of the most powerful minds the world has ever seen had devoted themselves to the earnest investigation of these questions: What is man? Whence came he? Whither is he going? The nature of God, the working of Providence, and the fate of man; and the result is declared in Scripture. Man by wisdom knew not God. Never did grosser darkness brood o'er the surface of society than at the time Christ came. The voice of philosophy had been hushed, poetry had been degraded, confidence in gods and men had been lost. The Gnosis of the period was a miserable hash of the old Greek learning and the Persian magic. It was an age of atheism and superstition and an age of audacious and unblushing vice. The old virtue had passed away with the old belief, and luxury and lust had taken its place. It was, moreover, an age of deep and settled sadness. Pilate's sneering question to our Lord, "What is Truth?" was but the echo of the world's half-despairing cry. In answer to this world's cry, Christ said, "I am truth." He was the Teacher sent from God; and as the heavens are high above the earth, so is He above all other teachers. He not only tells us more extraordinary things, but in manner He is altogether different. He speaks as if the region of eternal truth were His native home. Even old truths, as they fall from His lips, receive a spiritual glow and glory which give them new power. Every truth, as it falls from Him, commends itself to our truest and deepest nature. We feel that it is not only a truth, but germ of infinitely more truth, that, like the segment of a circle, which enables us to describe the whole circle itself, it is part of a glorious Unity, drawing up our souls to the perception of the Unity itself.

He is not only the great Teacher of Truth, He is the Truth itself—the Truth incarnate. His whole life is the Divine utterance. His doctrine has been drawn out into the events of a life history. And how much has Christ taught the world in this way! In fact, it has never been the same world since Christ lived in it. A kind of celestial consciousness has taken possession of it. He, the living truth, has been lifted up above us, drawing all men unto Himself. He has taught us the true nature of God by living out in human moulds the perfections of Deity. "He that hath seen Me hath seen the Father." What a truth was given to the world in that one declaration! God such an one as He whom we see dwelling among men as man, sitting at our tables, healing our diseases, pitying our infirmities, weeping at our tombs—the same tender, compassionate Being whom we see meeting the lonely family at Bethany, and saving the wretched woman from the pitilessness of her accusers! No longer does the image of cold, incompassionate Deity arise in our hearts when we kneel and say, "Our Father," but of a living, loving, thinking Being like ourselves—of the infinite loving-kindness that broods o'er the whole human family, desiring to lift them up into blessed companionship and likeness to Himself.

He hath taught us also the true nature of man, by fulfilling the idea of our perfect manhood, by holding up to us our own nature complete and glorious, by showing what we might be if true, and what we are not, because untrue. He has come that we might have life, and that more abundantly —life in its deepest and fullest sense—in the setting of our whole nature to its highest standard, and the development of every part to its most glorious issue. He does this not only by holding up the image of faultless beauty. If this were all, despair could be our only portion. As we gaze upon its supreme sanctity amid our earthliness and imperfection, we might well give up all hope. But in the knowledge of the Lord Jesus Christ there is not only the promise, but the power, of this new and better life. " The wages of sin is death, but the gift of God is eternal life in the Lord Jesus Christ." He Himself is the seed-form within the soul—the germ of the everlasting growth. He frees us from the crushing weight of our sin, from the overmastering law of disorder, and calls us to go forward with Himself upon the everlasting path. " Because I live, ye shall live also."

(a) The knowledge of Christ must be personal.—It follows, then, from these reflections that the knowledge of the Lord Jesus Christ must be personal. It is not simply the knowledge of so many dogmas, but of a living person. He is the beginning and the end of all our knowledge. In Him are we to begin, continue, and end. Let us look to Him as the author and as the finisher of our faith, and how great is the sphere for growth opened out in Him! Whilst the tender child may come to the knowledge of Christ in its initial stage, the ripest saint will be still reaching forth unto Him. Beyond the creed, beyond the Church, beyond the conception of the most gifted and noble of our race, is Christ Himself. He ever calls us on from higher heights to

higher still. Much it is to be a son of God, much it is to have begun the high career, but to be such a son as Christ was, One whose doctrine was the Father's truth, One whose sacrifice was the Father's will, One whose inspiration was the Father's love! Obedience, goodness, lovingness, Christlikeness—this is the high calling set before us. Let us ever look to Him that we may catch the rays of the same excellence, that we may be His children by derivations of the same Spirit, and grow in His knowledge "till we all come in the unity of the faith and of the knowledge of the Son of God unto the perfect man, unto the measure of the stature of the fulness of Christ."

(b) This knowledge must be also. general.—But whilst the knowledge of the Lord Jesus Christ is, in the first place, personal, it is also general—in fact, universal. In Him consist all the treasures of wisdom and knowledge; and all knowledge, in so far as it is true knowledge, is part of the knowledge of the Lord Jesus Christ. All arts and sciences are but broken lights of the Great Light. Here also we have vast scope for growth. I wish that we Christians could always remember this. A most unnatural divorcement has been made between religious and secular knowledge. All knowledge should be religious—*i.e.*, it should be conducted in a religious spirit, with a distinctly moral aim and made helpful to the conquering of the world in the name and spirit of the Lord Jesus Christ. We should identify everything that ministers to the bettering of the world with the Lord Jesus Christ, and for His sake desire it. Agriculture and commerce and manufactures are but the continuation of the great miracles of feeding the thousands. In our hospitals, in our schools, and our sanitary measures we see the continuation of the miracles of healing. The personal presence that blessed Palestine has become a

diffused spirit in the world. The injunction, then, comes not only to the individual, but to governments and to nations, "to grow in the knowledge of the Lord Jesus Christ."

III.—Growth gradual and sure is the most desirable.

And now, finally, we come to the point whence we started. Growth is God's law in the kingdom of grace as in the kingdom of nature. Better the gradual and steady progress of Christian principle from childhood to youth, and from youth to manhood, and from manhood to old age, than that fitful life which has periods of indifference, agony, and revival. Better the steady life of faithfulness to duty within the father's home, represented by the elder son in the parable, than the folly of the prodigal and the joy of his return. Better for the promise of the future is the power of a habit that has been growing with the growth and strengthening with the strength, than even the glowing joy of the man suddenly arrested on a downward career. Thanks be to God, we can turn to Him in our sorest extremity—even when the world casts us off. But let no man make the dangerous experiment. Human experience tells us that a man dies as he lives. And even when a man does turn to God with strong purpose and endeavour after new obedience, the chains and fetters of his old habits heavily weight him. Sin and vice cannot all at once leap to the rewards of continuous piety and habitual virtue. Be it therefore our effort and our prayer that we and our children may "grow in grace and in the knowledge of the Lord Jesus Christ." By small stages every day, rather than occasional forced marches, are we to reach the Kingdom; by small acts of service oft repeated, rather than by splendid sacrifices are

E

we to note our progress. Let us value as the most priceless blessings the means of grace—our Bibles, our sacraments, and our churches, which receive our children in the name of the Lord Jesus Christ, which grow them in the image of the Lord Jesus Christ, and hold out to them constantly the blessed hope of everlasting life of growth and grace and beauty; and that even when they have erred and wandered from the way like lost sheep, proclaim pardon to penitents through the mercy of God in Jesus Christ.

IV.—There is another growth possible.

Lastly—Let us be warned. There is set before us the possibility of another terrible growth—nay, the assurance that if we are not growing in grace towards life eternal, we are growing in deformity towards death eternal. We are either purifying our souls with the hope of the Gospel, or soiling them beyond all hope of cleansing. With what alarm we mark the inroads of disease upon the body; but with how much greater alarm should we regard disordering of the soul! Men weep when the body dies; when it is borne to its last resting place, they follow it with sad procession; but there is no token of mourning over the sadder calamity of the dying soul. Why is this? If you should find even some statue of beautiful proportions and wondrous inspiration cast from its pedestal, lying upon its face on the ground, shattered, disfigured, and soiled in the mire, you would mourn over the desecration. You would say, What lost wealth! What wasted labour! Into this marble, genius wrought its energies and breathed its living soul; and now it lies there thrown down and trampled upon. But ah! what is this to the living man that has fallen from his high position? God wrought in that man His own image. He breathed into that man His own nature. He sent Him into the world, not to be as a mere statue, a dull and motionless shape, but to be a growing and exhaustless force. Realms of infinite truth and beauty burst open before him; the possibilities that await every soul born into the world crowded on his right hand and his left. But the world challenged him, and he fell. He wrested from its true bias a nature made for heavenly ends; he has made all base which was all beautiful in God's design. Affections that might have been sweet and pure as angels, have been soured and turned to wrath; the dread authority of reason has been defied, and the sublime sanctity of conscience set at nought; until now the spirit shares the rottenness of the bones and is soaked into the corruption of the flesh. This downward growing is something to weep and mourn over. Poverty and affliction are sad things; but there is no such poverty as poverty in affection and truth and virtue. There is no such affliction as the wresting of a soul away from God and goodliness and grace. There is no such death as the death of a soul.

BEHOLD! I STAND AT THE DOOR AND KNOCK.

"BEHOLD! I STAND AT THE DOOR AND KNOCK. IF ANY MAN WILL HEAR MY VOICE, AND OPEN THE DOOR, I WILL COME IN TO HIM, AND WILL SUP WITH HIM, AND HE WITH ME."—*Rev. iii. 20.*

(Preached on the Re-opening of Blackfriars, after being closed for repairs, August, 1890.)

SOME of you will have seen the picture of the great artist, Holman Hunt, representing this scene. There is an Oriental dwelling, in great part concealed from view by the contiguous shrubs and luxuriant flowers. These obscure and darken the dwelling. In the midst of these there is a door closed, and before it there stands the figure of the Light of the World— the thorny cross upon the brow and the lantern in hand. In journeying through this world's ways and by-ways, enlightening and gladdening, He has come to this darkened dwelling with the expectation of entrance and of fellowship. He has knocked before, and His hand is again upon the door. At first sight there is the vivid expectation of entrance. "It cannot be that they have not heard." As we gaze the expression changes. There comes upon the face the expression of regret that there is so long a pause; and as the pause continues, and the conviction comes that the inmate cannot or will not hear, it is the expression of pain. You can discern with what bitterness He is about to turn away.

As you look, you are led to ask the question—"Why was the door not opened to that gentle Visitor?" Was it that within the dwelling there was a busy mother, so intent upon her household duties, preparing for the return of husband and children, that she feared the loss of time by opening the door to this stranger? or was there within a workman bending so eagerly over his bench, and so deftly plying his noisy tools, that he did not hear it? or, had we been on the other side, would we have seen an aged man reading, with book in both hands, so intent upon the events and characters of times gone by, that he had no ear for the sounds of the present? or was there a miser there, gazing greedily upon his gains, and afraid to open, lest he might be forced to part with them? or were there within some engaged in a game of Oriental hazard, heedless to all except the chances of the lot as it fell? or were the inmates of the household so bent upon mirth and joy that, amid music and dancing, they heard not and heeded not the knocking at the door? This might easily be. I went last year to a house in the country, to make a call of friendship. It was a bright evening at the close of an early harvest. I knocked at the door, and knocked again. As I stood, I came to understand the reason why my call was unheeded. A company was assembled, and a joyous feast was going on. I could hear their mirth, but they heard not me. That did not matter much. But pleasure may become a hindrance. The song of mirth may drown the voice of that blessed Visitant who stands without and pleads for admission, and then it does matter; for He who knocks at our door has eternal life at His disposal. "Hear, and your soul shall live," is the Voice Divine.

As we pause and meditate, another thought enters. Is it grief that has closed the door? A widow sits gazing upon the face of him that loved and cherished her, now stiffened in death. She nurses her solitary grief. All she wants is to be alone, and thus excludes the only One that could comfort her and bring light into her darkened dwelling.

Nay, darker thoughts are suggested. Is this the abode of vice and crime? Do these walls and this closed door conceal the harlot and her guilty companion, or the company of robbers dividing their unhallowed gains? Unwelcome would be the entrance of this holy Visitant; and yet He is the only one who could lift thém up and give to them enduring happiness. To them—even to them—His heart is filled with yearning love. With what pain—excluded—He turns away!

We know not—for, as yet, the artist has not given us the companion picture, showing us the other side of the closed door—but this we know, that all through the ages these and like causes have hindered the Saviour's entrance. Vice and crime will have nought to do with Him, although He has come to seek and to save that which was lost. Selfish greed and selfish pleasure have locked the gates of the heart against Him. Earthly joy and earthly sorrow have often left the Saviour at the door. The learning of the world hath often despised the wisdom that cometh down from above; and men, by intense occupation, and women, by all-engrossing ministration, have allowed Him to pass away, who alone could have brought to them the blessing that maketh rich and the peace that the world cannot give.

We have a specimen here in the Church of Laodicea. It was a prosperous city. It was eminent also as a Christian city. The Gospel had found ready entrance and made rapid progress. It was rich, and increased with goods. In many other places the Christian Church was in a struggling condition—under the ban of public opinion and sometimes under persecution—but not here. It was a most respectable

Church. "They had need of nothing." There was no congregational anxiety. Their ecclesiastical organization seems to have been complete. They were a model Church, so far as outward machinery was concerned. Very high praise is given in this respect—"I know thy works." But they were "works" without the soul of life. There was much congregational activity, while real indifference had set in—a Christian Church with Christ outside. They had all the things that were Christ-like inside with Christ Himself left out. Is not this a picture of much of the ecclesiasticism of the present day? It reads like the annual report of the secretary and treasurer, rehearsed with smiling lips, to a comfortable and satisfied people. "We are glad to say that the finances have been well maintained during the last year. The stipend has not only been maintained, but has received an addition. The contributions to the Home Mission Fund have not diminished, and those to the Foreign Mission are satisfactory. The organization has been maintained with its well-known efficiency; and, in addition to former mission and Sabbath school works, there has been added a young men's guild." Works! all works! Organization, but little real life; a mechanical grind of religious affairs, without real religion; a skeleton of courts and societies and such like, without the pulsing blood and the glowing vitality; a kind of religious fussiness, with Christ left outside. How true is it, as an old writer says: "A man may hide himself from the Lord amid the forms of the Church as well as among the trees of the Garden."

This rich Laodicean Church, so well pleased with itself, was an abomination to the Lord. "I will spue thee out of My mouth." How sad! In some things they were far up. They are free from faults of doctrine. They are not charged with the errors of the Nicolaitanes, nor with the seductions of Jezebel; but they are neither cold nor hot, and Christ is outside — like many churches now. Sound in doctrine, reformed in service, free from gross faults—not at all like the lapsed masses, but models of propriety—and yet they are that to Him they are professing to serve. And why? Because He is outside who ought to be inside. He is at the circumference who ought to be at the centre. He, the Lord, is nowhere, where He ought to be all in all. What we want is more of Christ, and less of ecclesiasticism; more of the holy and beautiful Nazarene, and less of controversy; more of the Spirit of the Lord, and less of our machinery; more life, more love, more fellowship with the Master—to receive Him into our heart of hearts, and to make Him our joy, our crown, our glory.

(1) This picture suggests the nearness of Christ. How near the Son of God has come to us! He is the Son of Man. He is bone of our bone and flesh of our flesh. He is our brother. He knows all our hopes and fears. He knows our temptations and our sorrows. He was in the wilderness alone, tempted of the devil. He wept with sorrowing sisters beside a brother's grave. He was in agony because of our sin. How closely He comes to every human heart! As closely as the sun to every flower, as closely as the light to every human eye.

(2) And yet how far off He is kept! At the door. The sunlight travels far in its course from high heaven; and though it has travelled so far, yet it is in my power, by shutting the door of my eye, the thin film of flesh, to keep out that light, and to remain in darkness. And that Light, "the Light of Life," travelled so far—from the very throne of God—and I may keep out that Light and abide in darkness! Oh, wonder of wonders! The Saviour's condescending love and man's self-destroying blindness! One

wonder is, that the man keeps the Visitor at the door; and the other is, that this Visitor, kept at the door, does not straightway leave. But no. He waits in expectation. He knocks, and knocks again and again.

(3) The third suggestion is, the joy of fellowship. "Behold! I will come in and sup with him, and he with Me." The supper is essentially suggestive of fellowship. The breakfast is the meal suggestive of preparation for the work of the day; the dinner of refreshment amid the tasks of the day; but the supper, when the work of the day is over, when there is the period of rest, and the soul is free, is the scene of fellowship and joy. How often have we experienced this! But in Christ there is a higher joy and a sweeter fellowship and more enduring benefit. Open the heart to Him, and He will come in and sup with you, and you with Him. There will be spiritual intercourse, more free and hearty; more enlargement of the heart; more glorious hopes enkindled; more of life, real life—life that is truly glorious.

He is knocking continually—knocking at the door of many hearts for entrance—and knocking at the door of other hearts for freer entrance and freer fellowship.

He is the Lord of all Nature, and He has made all this so fair! Through all this beauty He knocks at the door of our hearts, and one wonders that all do not break out into the loud benediction — "Praise God, all creatures here below!" Yet there are eyes that cannot see and ears that cannot hear. What indifference to the Lord of all this life and beauty!

He knocks in Providence. Have you not the memory of times when He was near you—that time when your earthly hope was broken—that dark night when the light of your eyes was removed?

He knocks in the ordinances of His Church. Have there not been times when, in the quiet sanctuary, you heard His voice—sweet communion seasons that you can never forget?

Still He knocks!

All things knock at closed human hearts for the admission of their Lord. Life and Death, angels, principalities, and powers, things present and things to come, height and depth, and every other creature, unite in one long, loud cry: "Awake, thou that sleepest, and arise from the dead, and Christ shall give thee light."

> Oh, Jesus, Thou art pleading,
> In accents meek and low:
> "I died for you, My children;
> And will ye treat Me so?"

> Oh, Lord, with shame and sorrow,
> We open now the door.
> Dear Saviour, enter, enter!
> And leave us nevermore.

THE LORD IS GREAT.

"THE LORD IS GREAT, AND GREATLY TO BE PRAISED: HE IS TO BE FEARED."—*Psalm xcvi. 4.*

(Re-Opening of Blackfriars after Renovation of Organ.)

A GREAT statesman was on one occasion asked what had been his profoundest life-thought. He was one who had read poetry and philosophy, was an authority in literature and in law, had listened to eloquent men expressing their loftiest sentiments, and had no small part in shaping the destiny of his nation. He paused for a second or two in reflection, and said: "The profoundest thought of my life was my personal responsibility to God." And this is true. The thought of God is both a restraint and an encouragement — the profoundest factor in the elements of life. Nations and individuals rise and fall according to their thought of God.

In New York there was a celebrated Scottish preacher— Dr. Ormiston. His church was crowded every Sabbath in that city, where it is not easy to fill churches. And why? Not because he had any tricks of manner or language, for he was a plain man, using plain words. The peculiar feature of attraction was well described by a lady member: "I like to hear Dr. Ormiston. He makes me feel that God is so big." This is my feeling always in reading these Psalms. He makes us feel that God is a real being and so great. He is to be had in reverence of all that are about Him.

"God is our refuge and strength, a very present help in trouble. Therefore will not we fear, though the earth be removed, and the mountains cast into the sea."

"According to Thy name, O God, so is Thy praise unto the ends of the earth. Thy right hand is full of righteousness."

"This God is our God for ever and ever: He will be our guide even unto death."

"Be Thou exalted, O God, above the heavens: let Thy glory be above all the earth."

"Thou art the God that doest wonders. Thy way is in the sea, and Thy path in the great waters, and Thy footsteps are not known."

"All the gods of the nations are idols: but the Lord made the heavens. Honour and majesty are before Him: strength and beauty are in His sanctuary."

This feeling of the greatness of God, the mighty Spirit beyond the bended heavens, has been realised in all nations and in all religions. The Jews led off in this respect. God was great and God was near. His voice was the storm; and the tides ran away at the frowning of His countenance. The one element of greatness has been intensely realised by the Mohammedans. Every night, in every village and city, from Gibraltar to furthest India, do you hear the cry of the sentinel from his lone post: "Allaho Akbar! Allaho Akbar! Allaho Akbar!"—God is great! God is great! God is great!

It has been usual to illustrate the greatness of God by dwelling upon the great scenes in Creation and the great Providential events in history. As we think of this and all the bright worlds above called into being by Him; as, bending in silent awe and looking up to those myriad orbs that look down upon us as the very eyes of God, we cannot help exclaiming, "Great and marvellous are Thy works,

Lord God Almighty! Who shall not fear Thee, O God, and glorify Thy name, for Thou only art holy?" Still, I think that our sense of the greatness of God is more intense when we come to examine the very smallest of His works—the minute cells of the growing plant, or the marvellous adaptation of means to ends in the smallest animals. Let any man reverently examine these things, with the aids of modern science, and he will be inclined to exclaim, "Wonderful! Wonderful!" at every turn. And even these bear no more proportion to the greatness of God than the spark bears to the flame it creates. He is great beyond all our conceptions of greatness. Perhaps we find the truest pointer stars to the greatness of God in the lives of truly great and good men among us. God has made man in His own image, and man at his best is the highest index of God. He is the high priest of Creation; and all his powers of intellect and heart, all his aspirations and accomplishments, sanctified by the lights of the Word and of the Spirit, best speak to us of God. Therefore did the Word become flesh and dwell among us. "And we beheld His glory, the glory as of the only begotten of the Father, full of grace and truth."

"God is greatly to be feared." There are two kinds of fear—slavish fear and filial fear.

I was once speaking to the son of a great man distinguished in letters. He was in trouble. He had got into debt and among sharpers. I said to him: "You should tell your father." "Oh, I could not do that! My father is so big, and so far up from us, that scarcely would a child of his enter his room unless by arrangement." What a pity! What is fame or name to fatherhood? His children were more to him than all his writings, and all he would ever make by them. They had a slavish fear of him. I knew another—the son of an author equally distinguished. He said: "I would rather sit with my father than any one I know. I would rather talk with him, and I would rather tell him my troubles. He is so wise and he is so good."

There were the two kinds of fear. I need not tell you the results. The one led to ruin; the other to character and success. We have spoken of the Mohammedan cry, "God is great." Too exclusively have they fixed upon that one element. They are dwarfed thereby. It has led to a dead fatalism. The element lacking in their religion is the Incarnation. They have never realised how truly human God is—how near He is to them in all their toils and tears. They need the revelation of God in Christ. The worship is too exclusively that of slavish fear. "Allaho Akbar" is their only cry. They have not seen the face of God in Jesus Christ. There is no voice of joy; there is no element of gladness and praise in their religious services. God is great, and greatly to be feared; but also greatly to be praised, for He is our Father, our Friend, our Brother in Jesus Christ.

"The fear of the Lord is the beginning of wisdom." Yes, when we fear God we realise what sin is; and when this fear leads to Him for pardon and for strength, it leads us to fear Him in that higher sense. So that it is the beginning of wisdom, and also the end of wisdom. "Fear God and keep His commandments, for this is the whole duty of man." It becomes a jubilant, exultant element that passes into all our life, making all our obedience a joyous service.

What is the most priceless element in life? The fear of God. If you had a son going away from your home—a darling boy, in whose smile and voice you had oft rejoiced, what possession would you rather he had? Education? Knowledge? It is most valuable and easily carried, but alas! often perverted. Wealth? Well, it is a power, but it may so easily be scattered; nay, wealth itself may become a snare. What would you rather he had for character and comfort, for successful life here and a bright destiny? Well, I take it, that fear of God which is the beginning, the continuance, and the end of wisdom.

"The Lord is great, and greatly to be praised: He is to be feared."

HE KNEW WHAT WAS IN MAN.

"HE KNEW WHAT WAS IN MAN.—*John ii. 25.*
(*Preached in Blackfriars at Opening of East-End Exhibition.*)

WE have all heard this text quoted in a bad sense, as if it referred only to the deceit and vileness within our humanity. In this sense it is certainly true. We do not know the depths of our corruption. But that is not the whole truth. It refers also to the possibilities of good that are within our humanity. Christ knew by sad experience the hypocrisy and hellish passions of men, but He knew also, as no other ever knew or ever conceived before He came, the virtue and angelic grace to which man may rise. It was on these He set His heavenly eye. It was for the development and strengthening of these He came to earth. It was for the ripening and consummation of these that He died on Calvary. "Christ loved the Church and gave Himself for it, that He might sanctify and cleanse it with the washing of water by the Word, that He might present it to Himself a glorious Church, not having spot or wrinkle or any such thing." That was the aim—our humanity at its best, glorified and beautiful.

As the mother gazes upon her sleeping babe, her thoughts stretch out and are projected to the future. She wonders what is *in* the child, and prays that what is best within the child may be brought out to the greatest advantage.

Occasionally the dark thought of evil possibilities may enter her heart—latent vices that may yet destroy these graceful features, and passions that may course violently through that gentle form. But she puts these speedily aside. The picture on which she dwells constantly and lovingly is that of her boy going forth, full of promise, into the ranks of life, strengthening in virtue as he grows in years, maintaining his honour untainted and his word unbroken, gaining the respect of those around him, and rising into honour and success — kind to herself, and gentle and generous to all. For this she prays, and for this she ministers to him daily. This thought makes all hard work easy, and all her sacrifice a joy. This is her thought of what is in him, and of what may be brought out of him. And so Christ knew and thought of what was in man. He knew what was in man far better than ever mother knew what was in her child. He knew his divine origin and his eternal destiny; and He thought of a future—in its glory and beauty inconceivable by mortal man. He knew what was in man, and He came to bring it out. He is not only Emancipator, but Educator, calling upon all men to be His disciples.

There are two kinds of teachers. There are those who, well-informed themselves, pour their stores of knowledge freely out before their pupils. They endeavour to put as much *in* to them as possible. There are others who only try to bring out what is already there, to strengthen the faculties, and to lead them out to their proper objects—to stimulate the minds of those committed to them, and make them try to find out for themselves. I need not tell you which mode is best. "Education," in its original and truest sense, means a "drawing out" of that which is already in the mind. And so Christ deals with His disciples—His pupils. He knows what is in them; and, by His continual

F

ministry, endeavours to draw it out to best advantage. For what, brethren, does Christ live? For what is the Church, and ordinances, and all religious instruments? Simply to bring out, to the glory of the Father and to the good of the world, that which is in us. As we are very definitely reminded by the Apostle Paul: "And He gave some, apostles; and some, prophets; and some, evangelists; and some, pastors and teachers; for the perfecting of the saints, for the work of the ministry, for the edifying of the body of Christ: till we all come in [*into*] the unity of the faith, and of the knowledge of the Son of God, unto a perfect man, unto the measure of the stature of the fulness of Christ."

As the traveller wanders through any of our older countries he occasionally comes, in some sequestered spot, to the ruin that has been the keep of some powerful baron or the abode of fair women. All around is bare and barren. Thorns and weeds now rise through the broken floor. Time's tooth has eaten into the very walls themselves. The ancient ornaments are all defaced. Slimy things creep and crawl in the chambers where beauty sat once enshrined. But as the visitor wanders through its deserted rooms, the spirit of the past comes back upon him. He casts his eye back through the rolling centuries and beholds the scene of former times once more renewed, when the nobles lived there in their glory, when these broken walls stood sure and firm, when sounds of mirth arose around the festive board, when the joyous inmates threaded the mazes of the stately dance within its capacious walls. He can see its fair proportions once more renewed, and hear the voice of song proceeding from its now deserted bower. And it was with something of the same feeling that the Lord Jesus Christ looked upon our humanity. He beheld it as a ruin, but the ruin of what greatness! Its powers broken by the wear and tear of sinful ages, unholy passions coursing riotously through the chambers of the heart, selfish, sensual desires defiling with their slimy touch its heavenly aspirations. But as He thus surveyed our humanity in ruin there was present to His mind the thought of its pristine beauty and infinite capacity. He saw it once more renewed and purified from all its foulness; He saw all heavenly graces moving peacefully within it, instead of those unholy gusts of passion and of hatred; He saw the pleasing emotions of faith and love and hope and joy filling up the now deserted chambers of the soul. He saw within man the lines of possible beauty, the germs of sturdy virtue; He saw him no longer fallen, no longer steeped in sense and sin, but standing erect and firm, his face towards heaven, his soul radiant with holy beauty. And thus, gazing upon our humanity, He loved it and gave Himself for it, redeemed it with His own precious blood, and said: "My brothers, children with Me of a common Father—Forward to your true life! The power of endless being now is yours. The Spirit of God now is yours. The possibility of eternal growth now is yours. Behold in Me thy dignity and thy destiny! Follow Me! Follow Me! He that followeth Me shall not walk in darkness, but shall have the light of life."

A modern writer says: "When I was a little boy, a poor sculptor had a shed in my mother's backyard, where he worked all the day with mallet and chisel on marble. It was a great delight for me to watch him at his work. One day there was hauled into this rude studio an unusually large piece of marble—uneven, ragged, soiled. When I next visited the studio he was standing by it, his hand resting affectionately on it, as though he were in love with it. I remember how fondly he gazed upon it, as though looking into its very centre. At length I asked him, 'What are you going to do with that?' 'With that? Ah!' he said, 'there is a beautiful angel in that marble, and I am going to bring it out. In a month or so you will see how beautiful it is'—and then resumed his intent gaze upon the block of marble. By-and-bye I came to understand what he meant by the 'angel in the marble.'" This represents the attitude of Christ before our humanity. It was a rough block. We have only to read ancient history, with its barbarous wars and heathenish orgies, or to look to the shady side of our modern life, to realise how dark it was and is. But there He stands, His hand upon that rough block; and ever since He entered our world the angel in our human nature has been more and more revealed.

What a wonderful power He had in the days of His flesh of touching that which was best in others around Him! You know the different influence some people have upon you. There are some who bring out the angel that is within you. In their presence you are clothed with purity, you have heavenly desires, you are filled with love to all mankind. There are others who seem to arouse whatever of the devil there is within you. You just long to contradict them, and to curse humanity at the same time. But Christ ever touched the best springs of the heart. You remember his interview with the sinful Samaritan woman. He knew what was in her, notwithstanding her chequered career. He saw the angel within the woman, and spoke to it; nay, He made it speak, though it had been dumb for many a day before. "Is not this the Christ?" she said to her companions. And so, too, of the disciples. They were not much to begin with; but they were great men after discipleship with Him. John, the fire-eater, became John, the gentle; Peter, the unstable, became Peter, the Rock; and James, the zealot, became James, the just; and so on through all the history of the Church. Every conversion is just an illustration of how Christ knew what was in man, and how to bring it out. In every right thought and pure desire Christ is with us and Christ is for us.

In this, Christ is different from many modern reformers and many modern preachers. They begin at the outside; He begins in the inside. They delight in the denunciations of that which is evil; He gives the sweet picture of that which is pure and holy and pleasing unto the Father in heaven. Their proposals are laws of restraint and negation; His are the promises, nay, the prophecies, of grace and of goodness.

Let us come to Him. Let us learn of Him who was meek and holy. Let us cast ourselves upon Him for our own salvation and for the salvation of those around us. We will be successful in so far as we imitate Him in this respect. Let us speak to the angel within the man. So long as you look only upon that which is worst in a man, and rail against it, you only harden him. But if, in a large, loving, sympathetic nature, you seize upon that which is best; if you can strike the sweet chord of his nature; if you can touch the secret springs of goodness, there is no measuring of the influence for good which you may have. Say to the one who has lost reputation and position: "Man! it is in you yet to be honest;" say to him who has been drunken: "Man! it is in you yet to be sober;" say to him that is far down: "Man! it is in you yet to rise up," and your words will give courage and hope, will lead to aspiration and to effort.

"For the grace of God that bringeth salvation hath appeared to all men, teaching us, that denying ungodliness and worldly lusts, we should live soberly, honestly, and godly in this present world; looking for that blessed hope and the glorious appearing of the great God and our Saviour Jesus Christ."

HE THAT RULETH HIS SPIRIT.

"HE THAT RULETH HIS SPIRIT IS BETTER THAN HE THAT TAKETH A CITY."—*Proverbs xvi. 32.*

(After close of the War in the Soudan.)

THE taking of a city is a great matter. The capture of ancient Troy has been the theme of Homer's glorious song. The taking of Tyre by Alexander the Great, after a seven months' siege, was the story and the boast of centuries. In the stones brought up from the ruins of ancient Nineveh we find depicted the elaborate preparations and the varied instruments for the taking of a city, the towers from which they threw into it the javelins, the battering rams with which they attacked the walls and doors, the catapults which they threw over the walls, and the devices by which they dug beneath them. Something of this we have known also in modern days. Many of us remember the relief of Lucknow. The wild Sepoys had taken the city. The devoted garrison, protecting the women and children, was bravely holding out, under Generals Havelock and Outram, in the Residency, within the north-west wall, with 4,700 men and 32 guns, when the great commander, Lord Clyde, hurried to their rescue. Storming the Dilkoola Palace, he enabled Sir Henry Havelock and Sir James Outram and their forces to come out free, and assist in storming the other portions of the city. The meeting of Sir Colin (Lord Clyde) with the other two generals, when our beleagured army was about the point of despair, is one of the most dramatic scenes in the history of our country. In our Corporation Galleries there is a painting in which the scene is depicted. There are the three central figures—Sir Colin, General Havelock, and General Outram. The character and rugged strength are marked in the Scottish chieftain's face; while the anxiety and suffering, which Havelock has gone through, are finely revealed in the countenance of that Christian gentleman, who, in gladness and in gratitude, is clasping both of his deliverer's hands in his. With uncovered head stands, looking on, with radiant face, General Outram. Major, now General Sir Archibald Allison, Sir Colin's private secretary, stands near his illustrious chief; while in that brilliant circle of warriors are also seen General Wyndham, Sir John Inglis, Sir Hope Grant, and Captain, now Field-Marshal Lord Wolseley. In the foreground are some dead Sepoys, and also several wounded Highlanders, who, though nigh unto death, are raising their arms feebly in salutation to that beloved chief. It is a touching picture, and commemorates the taking of a city, in which there is not only the glory of power, of skill, of ardent endeavour and bravery, but the glory of merciful purpose, the deliverance of the weak and the helpless. With what welcome he was received at home! And yet, after all, the wise man says: "He that ruleth his spirit is better than he that taketh a city." The scene of outward pomp and power is contrasted with that within the heart, which no man can witness. The mighty commander and confused noises of the battlefield are contrasted with the quiet thoughts and volitions of the soul. How different! Instead of swords and spears, there are prayers, and sometimes tears. Instead of prancing horses and moving men, there are the subtle, unseen movements of the quick spirit.

"He that ruleth his spirit is better than he that taketh a

city." There is here the intimation of a war that has ever been going on between the elements of good and evil within the man, of order and of chaos, authority and confusion. The old Gnostic idea was that human nature and the world were thoroughly bad things; that the only way to get quit of evil was to escape from the world entirely, and to kill off every natural affection and desire. The philsophers enjoined a life of seclusion and self-abnegation. Many of them retired to the groves and the cells and became anchorites — weak and useless creatures, caricatures of humanity. Human nature as it came from the hand of God is a whole — a beautiful whole. Not any part of it is to be exterminated, any more than our arms and legs are to be cut off. The desires and appetites by which we are linked to the world, as well as the thoughts and aspirations by which we are united to God, all have their true place and purpose in this being as designed by God; and our duty is not to ignore them, but rule them from the throne of power within—the living spirit—and to establish, in place of wild confusion, peace and concord. As it is put even more expressively in the New Testament (Gal. v. 16): "Walk in the Spirit, and ye shall not fulfil the lust of the flesh. For the flesh lusteth against the Spirit, and the Spirit against the flesh: and these are contrary the one to the other." If we live in the Spirit, let us also walk in the Spirit.

Better is he that ruleth his spirit than he that taketh a city; *first*,—because it is the assertion of power in a good cause; *second*,—because the battle is in the higher sphere of moral forces.

I.—IT IS THE ASSERTION OF POWER IN A GOOD CAUSE.

Battles have not always been gained nor cities taken in a good cause. Very wonderful are the retractions of history—

the verdicts of mankind upon the exploits of their ancestors. There never was such a holy war in semblance as that of the Crusaders. Millions marched forth, and yet we have discovered that it would have been just as well if they had stayed at home. For centuries our fathers fought on the Border for the possession of the city of Berwick, and now we grieve that so much good blood should have been shed in vain. We are even coming to think that the Crimean War need not have been waged, and that it would have been better for our country and for Europe if Alma, Inkerman, and Balaclava had never been heard of. But the ruling of the spirit in a right cause always leads to good result; it is the cause of order, and the result is lasting happiness. Some may think it an easy matter to rule the spirit, easier than to fly from the world altogether; but it is no such easy matter to abstain from that which is hurtful, and to use rightly and in moderation the things with which we must deal. For instance, if one has the tendency or habit of indulging to excess in strong drink, he must abstain altogether. This is the easiest, this is the best for him. It is a thirst set on fire of hell. His safety is in abstinence. The ruling of his spirit saves from destruction. And there are many spheres in which we must rule the spirit, not in avoiding our foes, but in meeting them bravely. We cannot avoid working at our work, that we and our dependents may be provided for; and yet this working at our work may so engross our attention that we may forget altogether higher interests. The only cure is self-government.

We cannot avoid mingling with our fellow-creatures; and yet, in doing this, our temper will be tried in a thousand ways, either through our weakness or the waywardness of others. Here also we must exercise self-restraint.

We cannot avoid seeking shelter, and food, and dress.

And yet in these we may be tempted to extravagance and needless luxury. How many, through pure heedlessness, are tempted into the miseries of debt, and into the degradation and the shifty, dishonest ways of debt. Here also we must rule the spirit.

The same in regard to recreations. These we need; but some would make life all a play. There is no high purpose before them; it is levity all the time. What is to be the standard here—the golden mean between asceticism on the one hand, and levity on the other? Just the remembrance of the purpose—recreation—the invigorating of the body and the mind for useful work. When anything wastes our strength, enfeebles the mind, or corrupts our soul, it is not recreation—it is dis-creation. Here is a sphere that emphatically calls for careful ruling of the spirit.

We can well understand why the wise king should have attached so much importance to the ruling of the spirit. Oh! the beauty of a well-balanced mind—a mind not under the government of intellect alone, or of sentiment alone, but a mind in which intellect is warmed by affection, and in which sentiment is guided by reason; the whole together—emotion, reason, intellect, and feeling, understanding and desire—the executive faculties, so to speak, and the legislative faculties, pervaded by loyalty to the Divine Sovereignty, and moving together to accomplish His will—a soul under government.

II.—Better is he that ruleth his spirit than he that taketh a city, for the battle is in the sphere of higher forces—the field of moral forces. It is interesting to behold a stout, thick-set, bull dog of a man lifting a great weight or breaking a chain with his fist; but how much better is it to see a gentle man, of fragile frame, holding on persistently to a beneficent purpose, or a strong man resisting the tide of rising temper under provocation. "Why do you speak so graciously to that man? He treats you rudely and speaks badly of you." "Why? Well, I would not like to be overcome by his rudeness." It is a heroic action to clamber up the ramparts under the fire and fight back the enemies on the summit in a hand-to-hand fight; but still more heroic is it to face an evil in ourselves or in others, and to fight till victory crowns the day. After all, it is more difficult. Many a one has stood well on the field of battle, where cannons to right of them, cannons to left to them, volleyed and thundered, that has completely broken down in the quieter ranks of life. Behold, out in a small island of the Atlantic, a remarkable man—now a prisoner there! He is wearing himself out in peevishness and jealousy—solaced by no great thoughts and sustained by no heroic spirit. Yet, this is the great conqueror of the modern time, the victorious taker of a hundred cities, one who made the whole civilised world shake with dread. But when he came to the place where true greatness could be manifested—in solitariness and suffering patience—he utterly broke down. He could not rule his spirit. Where many a Christian woman, many a gentle girl, would have shone forth by an all victorious patience, he utterly failed. He could take cities, but he could not rule his spirit.

The battle is in silence, often in solitariness, but it is not the less glorious; nay, it is thereby all the more glorious. The soldier will face the cannon's mouth, encouraged by the cheers of comrades; the general will undertake the difficult campaign, sustained by the sympathy and approval of a great nation; but here there is no place for ambition, no stimulus of passion, no sympathy of millions, to urge the victor on. In silence and in patience the battle is fought. No outward eye is gazing on the struggle. In the secret chambers of the soul the battle is fought. In his agony the disciple tastes the solitariness of the Master; no tongues to upbraid if he loses, no voices of applause if he wins. But the Father who seeth in secret shall openly reward, for hear the voice Divine: "To him that overcometh will I grant to inherit a crown of life."

If we would behold the highest kind of power in the highest sphere, we must look at another Conqueror. He was led as a lamb to the slaughter, yet He opened not His mouth. In the garden of agony we hear the prayer, "Not My will, but Thine be done." Apparently vanquished, He is the world's mightiest Victor. He hath spoiled principalities and powers, triumphing over them in His cross. As one has said: "He died on a cross, but He is a thousand times more alive than in the days of His flesh."

AND THOU SHALT BE MISSED.

"AND THOU SHALT BE MISSED, BECAUSE THY SEAT IS EMPTY."
—*1 Samuel xx. 18.*

(On the death of Mrs. John Tullis, of Inchcape.)

IT was the custom of the generals and the captains who had fought in the Peninsular War to meet once a year at the table of the Duke of Wellington in Apsley House upon the anniversary of Waterloo, the last and crowning victory in that great struggle. Here they renewed the memories of the heroic deeds in bygone years, and spake of those who had part in them. There was always a striking contrast between the former scenes and the present assembly, between the field of blood and the banqueting table, between the fierce conflict and the joyous feast; and yet, notwithstanding the contrast, there was one element of resemblance—*their ranks* were *always* being *thinned*. They had all known what it was on the field of battle, where shot and shell flew thickly around them, to see comrades falling at their side—often suddenly. And so, also, in the peace of the after years. At their assembly they often missed the presence or the voice that had been with them in the years before. Although no shot or shell now sped its fiery way among them, yet there were the flying arrows of death, ever calling one soldier after another from his station at the feast. I know not how many were at the first banquet, when the starred and medalled heroes met, when victory was fresh; but this I know, that as the years passed on, and the historic day recurred, it needed ever a shorter and a shorter table to receive the dwindling guests. Some who at first stood with martial bearing in the banquet hall, began to come with trembling limbs and stooping shoulders. The wrinkles gathered upon their wiry faces, the hairs whitened upon their foreheads, and the hands were shaky as they raised the wine-cup to pledge in silence the memory of their comrades who had fallen. The great hero was there, filling his place as host from year to year, but even he began to yield to the insidious enemy. At length, only a few old, old men kept coming to the familiar hall, and it became so sad, so unspeakably sad, to remember what they had been, and to gaze upon their present infirmities; to remember those who had been with them, and to behold their empty places in that great hall, that it was given up.

This, brethren, is the experience of all earthly companies. As our communion seasons recur, we miss many whose seats are now empty. As our anniversaries come round, the most suggestive voices are not from the lips that speak, but from those that are still. The place that knew them knows them no more; but God's kingdom is an everlasting kingdom: His dominion endureth throughout all generations. His Church depends not upon any company abiding in the same place. It is composed of the *whole company* in heaven and earth. Some have passed the flowing tide, and some are standing here. The members are ever changing locality, passing on from their lower earthly room into the higher rooms of the great Father's house. God's work—the great cause of righteousness and truth—depends not upon any, however great or good, abiding here. We and all others are simply the instruments for the time, and God's work shall go on though our hands drop off from it. This is a comfort.

The work ceases not with the workers. And there is this other comfort, that when the good are taken from us, their personal presence becomes a spiritual influence—a broader and a purer power for good. Surely if it had been good for anyone to have remained permanently upon the earth, it would have been Christ Himself, and, yet, He Himself declared that it was expedient for Him to go away. He Himself was missed in that early company of the disciples. No more did they gaze upon those benign features; no more did they hear the gracious words; no more follow Him as He went about doing good; but the personal presence became a universal power. His image was reflected in their hearts; His word germinated in their souls. He was more alive and mighty within them than ever. The feeble band became a conquering host. Against them were all the traditions and philosophies of the past, all the bigotry and cruelty of the time. Against them were kings, and armies, and principalities. There was brought to bear upon them all the horrors of the dungeon, the flame of the stake, the torture of the executioner, and the wild beast of the arena; but God was with them, and God was for them. The great blue heaven was their shield, and all the powers of the world were impotent against them. The power of Christ was made manifest by and through them. We would like to emphasize this thought to-day: God's work by and for the individual does not cease with the earthly departure.

I.—GOD'S WORK BY THEM DOES NOT CEASE.

"Thou shalt be missed, because thy seat is empty." This is true of all, whether we are young or old, poor or rich, big or little. Each individual fills up some little place, just as the parts of a machine, and not even one can fall out without affecting others. Even the poor wanderer by the wayside will be missed from his accustomed haunts, and by his gangrel companions. There are varied spheres, some broader and some narrower, and some where the gap seems more difficult to fill. A Newton, with wondrous capacity, masters the great law of the universe; a Wilberforce strikes off the chains of slavery, and gives freedom to thousands of his fellow-beings; a great soldier, like Wellington, stands in the terrible breach, and saves his country; or a great statesman, like Pitt, holds wisely the reins of power, and steers his nation safely through the desperate crisis. The void left by all such is great, and felt by a great number; but I question whether the sense of loss is one whit more intense than that which accompanies the individual taken from a narrower sphere; whether statesman, or soldier, or philsopher is more missed in their sphere, than the busy, ministering mother is missed by the household in which she ministered, or than the darling child withdrawn from the sorrowing parents. Nor does their influence cease with death. They rest from their labours, and their works do follow them. The departed hero becomes a living spirit among his countrymen, the sainted mother an abiding influence upon her household, and the tender child taken up attracts to heaven and to holiness. As we entered the Necropolis on Wednesday, and surveyed the many monuments of those who were once living among us, a gentleman stated that he had recently come from Italy, and asked why the Italians place lighted lamps upon the graves of their departed. They do this through the old belief that a light was often seen shining above the place where the good were buried. And this is true in a much higher sense. A light does indeed radiate from the tombs of those who have lived in Christ and died in Christ—the light of spiritual blessing and of gracious influence. They live more than ever in our affection, and they live in our faith. There are often earthly clouds that hide from us the excellence of those who are with us; so that it is not till the dear ones are taken from us that we entirely feel their value and appreciate their worth. The vision is loveliest at its vanishing away; and we perceive not fully until the parting that an angel hath been with us. How beautiful is the ministration by which the dead (as we call them) thus speak to us, thus help us, comfort us, guide us, and lift us up to better things! and it cannot be that the sainted dead thus speak to us in vain. Their memories are all around us; the traces of their footsteps are upon our paths; the memorials of them meet our eye at every turn; their presence is in our dwellings; their voices are in our ears; they speak to us in the sad reverie of contemplation, in the power of an abiding love, and in the bright light of hope; and it cannot be that they speak in vain.

II.—GOD'S WORK FOR THEM DOES NOT CEASE.

Jesus Christ said: "He that believeth on Me, though he were dead, yet shall he live;" "Because I live, ye shall live also." In Him death is the gate to higher work and purer joys. Here on earth everything ripens except man. The fruits ripen every year. A longer season would make them no bigger and no better. But what man ever came to full maturity? Even in the best and the greatest there are faculties not fully developed, affections not applied to the highest objects, and qualities unused. Are these never to ripen and do their highest work? Is there no sphere where the good and the gifted shall come to the perfection of their powers? The Scriptures and reason assure us that there is another brighter sphere in which they still live, and love, and serve the Father, with the powers trained so far upon the earth. They are as the plants of promise removed by death from the cold world to another more congenial, in which they will grow in beauty and in strength, and find sweet exercise of every function. Life, long or short, is but a waiting to be better born, and death is the birth angel. Otherwise, we cannot understand why useful lives are taken from us, and the useless ones often spared. The stroke of death must often seem more reckless than the lightning's flash, if there be no life for such hereafter. Consider this for a little in the light of our own experience. We have seen one die—the delight of his friends, the pride of his kindred; but he died. The fire of genius kindled in his eye, the generous affections of youth filled his heart, his foot was upon the threshold of life, his breast was filled with a thousand glowing, and noble, and never yet expressed aspirations; but he died. He died, while another of a nature dull, coarse, and unrefined; of habits low and base; of a life that had no promise in it but that of shame and misery, was suffered to live on upon our earth. Could this be if there were no other sphere for the gifted and the aspiring to act in? Can we believe that the energy just trained for action, the thought just bursting into expression, the deep passion of a noble nature just swelling into beautiful expansion should *never* unfold itself? Can we believe that all this should die, while every deformed and dishonoured power should live? *No.* Ye godly and glorious ones, ye Godlike in youthful virtue, ye die not in vain; ye teach us; ye assure us that ye are gone to some world of nobler life and action. The great and the *just* God has for you a higher service and higher joy. From that bright region they speak to us, and they say: "Sigh not in despair over the broken and defeated expectations of earth; sorrow not, as those who have no hope. Bear calmly thy lot in the faith of Him who died that we might live. Think, oh think of the mighty and glorious company that fill the immortal regions! Light, and life, and beauty, and holy work, and happiness are there. Hear the voice: 'Blessed are the dead who die in the Lord, for they rest'—they rest from their labours, and their works—works of piety, and love, and self-sacrifice, recorded in our hearts—do follow them." We miss them; miss them sadly as we look upon their empty seat—but let us remember that our irreparable loss is their eternal gain.

With these words, brethren, do I try to comfort myself and you in the sudden and great affliction that has fallen upon the household of our brother and upon the community. How deeply, how solemnly suggestive are these words in regard to her who came among us a beautiful and accomplished bride a few years ago. You know the brightness she carried in manner and person when she visited your homes. What she was in her own home is known only to him who was nearest to her, with whom we affectionately and deeply sympathise to-day. His is a sorrow with which no stranger can intermeddle. If the expression of human sympathy can afford any relief, it has been given by men and women of all classes, from the highest within our city; from friends of her family and of herself, far and near, down to even the obscure members of this district, who remember her brightness and her beneficence. Her memory will be long cherished by us all. I trust it will be sanctified to us all, and especially to the four little children who bear so strikingly her features. How short the time since I saw her pass my study window, on the last occasion she was out, with her stately figure and quick step. Little did I think that it was the last time I would look upon her. She knew the trial was before her—the trial that every mother has to undergo; but she faced it bravely and piously. Last Sunday, when we were assembled in the Sanctuary, the cloud overshadowed that home in which we were all interested; but we trusted and we prayed that it would pass by, and that the sufferer would be again among us, a beloved wife and a happy mother. Scarcely had the Sabbath passed, ere the tidings reached us of birth and of death, and of danger to wife and mother. Human skill, and a husband's love, and infant weakness, and true friendship stretched out their hands to save her for earth's duties and for earth's joys, but they could not. God has called her away. To us she seemed so well fitted and so much needed for life here; but God, in whose hands our breath is, has ordained it otherwise, and we bow our heads in woe; in faith, looking forward to the time when the broken families of earth shall be united in the mansions of heaven. We ask you earnestly to commend to the God of all comfort, the stricken husband. In the school of sorrow he will learn more than ever to minister to the sorrowful and heavy-laden. And those motherless children—may God guide them in all the trials, temptations, and experiences of the unknown future, and grant them and us a happy union in the kingdom of His glory! God grant us all grace to bend to the holy will of God in these dispensations. We, too, will be soon called upon to follow. He shall call, and we shall answer Him. Thanks be to God, who giveth us the victory through our Lord Jesus Christ. What hope can be so precious in this vale of tears as our hope in Him? And though in a short time our seat be empty also, and we be missed in the familiar home and in the sanctuary where we meet with brethren, our dear ones will not mourn as those who have no hope.

FAITH, HOPE, CHARITY.

"NOW ABIDETH FAITH, HOPE, CHARITY; BUT THE GREATEST OF THESE IS CHARITY."—*1 Cor. xiii.*

(*On return from holiday, September, 1858.*)

IN the whole range of literature there is nothing finer than this chapter of the Apostle. And this holds good not only in regard to the subject, but equally to the language in which the description is given. It has been named the Divine ode on Christian love. It is an evidence of the new nature of the Apostle in Jesus Christ. Not even from the lips of the Apostle John, whose theme is ever of love, has anything so beautiful come on the subject of Christian love. In the first part (1-4) charity is distinguished from other gifts. It is not mere glibness of speech nor clearness of perception, nor strength of conviction, nor abundant almsgiving, nor self-sacrificing patriotism. It is something deeper and better than all these. So much better, that without it, all these, or any of these, are as nothing. It is the stream of the Divine love in the human heart; the love of God in Christ, and the love of others in Him. All human love, such as that of mother towards child, the child's love to its parent, the love of friend for friend, are but faint reflections of this Divine love or charity. We have no word in our own or in any language that fully expresses it. Charity, in its modern sense, is too narrow; philanthropy is too cold. One writer has termed it the enthusiasm of humanity, but even this is too tame. The Apostle uses the Greek word "agapê;" but, as feeling how inadequate the word was, he goes on to describe it from the fourth to eighth verse. He gives what has been called the quinquagesima of charity—the fifteen manifestations: "Charity suffereth long, and is kind; charity envieth not; charity vaunteth not itself, is not puffed up, doth not behave itself unseemly, seeketh not her own, is not easily provoked, thinketh no evil; rejoiceth not in iniquity, but rejoiceth in the truth; beareth all things, believeth all things, hopeth all things, endureth all things."

On one of the brightest days in the Summer I went away back from the sea-shore among the hills of South Ayrshire with a friend. We wandered away up till we had left all human habitations far beneath us, and reached the mountain moor, where the cry of the plover and curlew alone broke upon the stillness; and there we came upon a beautiful spring, the fountain of the river that was winding through the valley beneath. Around the clear and sparkling spring there grew some of the most beautiful wild-flowers to be found in the district. This text was in my mind at the time, and here, I thought, was the symbol of charity. It is the spring of God's love rising up in the wilderness of earth. Within it and around it are the richest moral flora—long-suffering, kindness, brotherly love, humility, endurance, courtesy, gentleness; only there is this difference, "charity never faileth." The late Autumn will come, and these mountain flowers will become sere and yellow; the winter's frosts will come, and stem and petal and blossom, all will disappear; but no Autumn will ever touch the Divine spring of charity; no Winter's frosts will ever settle down upon its flowers and fruits. Those grand moral flora bloomed in the Paradise of God. As they bloomed in Paradise, so are they now with us; and as with us, so will they be with our children's children, for charity shall have an endless reign. This is the last thought of the Apostle, which he expounds from the eighth to the thirteenth verse. He compares it with other gifts in respect of permanence—with prophecies, with tongues, and with knowledge. Prophecies will be fulfilled, and pass away. The prophecy will become established fact. Tongues will cease. The old mother tongue of the world is now no more. The tongues of some of the natives of the South Pacific and of the North American tribes have ceased in our own day. We trust the day will come when English will alone be spoken throughout the bounds of the British Empire. In another respect tongues will cease. The tongues of eloquence and affection will become silent in death. The tongue of the Apostle himself is hushed on earth. The tongue of the preacher will be no longer heard. We often long for the touch of a vanished hand, and the sound of a voice that is hushed; but charity will never fail. Knowledge will pass away; that is to say, imperfect knowledge will merge into perfect knowledge, just as the knowledge of the child is lost in the knowledge of the man; but charity will never fail.

Then the Apostle adds: "Now abideth faith, hope, charity, these three; but the greatest of these is charity." This is not only the close, but the climax of the inspired ode. He brings the three sister graces together. He declares the permanence of the three, and asserts the pre-eminence of charity. We are not to understand that the Apostle in the least depreciates the other two graces; nay, much of what he has said about faith, might be said also about the others. Though I speak with the tongues of men and of angels, and have not faith, I am nothing. And though I have the gift of prophecy, and understand all mysteries, and all knowledge; and though I have all faith, so that I could remove mountains, and have not hope, I am nothing.

Why, then, does he declare charity to be the greatest?

There is a very beautiful explanation of this, which has lingered in the Church from the early ages. It has been said that faith and hope are needed only for an imperfect condition of things, but that love will be universal in the perfect. Faith is the evidence of things not seen, the substance of things hoped for; and that when we see as we are seen, when we know as we are known, faith will pass away into actual knowledge. We will then walk by sight, not by faith. It is said, also, that just as the stars are seen by the darkness of night, so hope is the star of the dark day here. It is the grace or quality that looks through to brighter realities. And that just as the bright light of the sun causes the stars to disappear, so will heavenly brightness exclude hope. All will then be so filled that hope will vanish. Now this is very beautiful. It has found such apt expression in the paraphrase that it will long hold possession of the heart of the Church.

> Faith, hope, and love, now dwell on earth,
>   And earth by them is blest;
> But faith and hope must yield to love,
>   Of all the graces best.
> Hope shall to full fruition rise,
>   And faith be sight above;
> These are the means, but this the end;
>   For saints for ever love.

This is in opposition to the express declaration of the Apostle: "Now *abideth* faith, hope, and charity." The word "abideth" is the very word used in the twelfth chapter of Hebrews, in contrast with the things which can be shaken. It is the very word of the thirteenth chapter of the same epistle: "Here we have no abiding city, but we seek that [abiding city] which is to come." The Apostle thus represents the three graces of faith, love, and hope as alike permanent—alike perpetual. That was not the distinction in his mind.

It is a mere assumption that faith and hope will perish with the mortal. Faith is strong confidence in God and in the things that are Godlike. A man by faith commits his his way unto the Lord, and is not afraid of evil. Faith, which is the sight of the invisible, makes him strong for endeavour, brave for conflict, patient in tribulation, calm in death. Setting God always before it, it endures and it dares, it works and it prays; toiler and sufferer, conqueror and martyr in one. Will faith, then, not be needed in heaven? Shall there be in heaven no heroism and no sacrifice, no ministry and no waiting, no service for God and Godlike ends, demanding faith? Shall we dare to say that the angels need not faith in those errands of ministration to God's world and to Christ's little ones? Shall we picture heaven as a state of passive quiescence, of luxurious reminiscence, with no enterprises of service and no heights of higher glory to be scaled? Then, and then only, can we contradict the saying, "There abideth faith."

And of hope—will it not also abide? What would human life be without hope? Shall hope, then, not enter the golden gates and walk the streets of pearl? Miserable conception! An immortality of stagnation; an eternity of monotony; all mine at once that shall ever be. No long, beautiful, boundless vista of perpetual growth in knowing and being. Nothing but an instantaneous, mechanical, stereotyped perfection. No! Christ will call us on from higher heights to higher still. All through the eternal ages we shall be ever going on from strength to strength, and adding grace to grace. At no point will the progress of the soul be arrested, but ever will hope bring to view the never-ending background of heavenly possibility. Hope will abide.

Now abideth faith, hope, charity, these three immortals; yet, of the three, love is the best and greatest, not because it abideth while the other two perish in the crossing of the dark river, but because, of all graces, love is likest God. It is His own name: God is love. "Beloved, let us love one another, for love is of God; and every one that loveth is born of God, and knoweth God. He that loveth not, knoweth not God, for God is love." Christ gave this truth its first full development in His life and death. He has made it the supreme grace. It is the beginning of Christian life; it is the very spirit of the life; the end of all Christian effort. It is the love of Christ warming the heart that gives strength to faith. It is the love of Christ presenting the boundless realm of good that inspires hope.

When a great structure is rising, there are multitudes of labourers. There are workmen in wood, and in stone, in iron, and other materials; and each in his own department is good and necessary. But higher than all is the architect. His authority brings all these workers together, directs their tasks, and gives to their skill a central unity—an end towards which they are all unconsciously tending; and from so many heads and hands, differing and independent, there emerges at last, under the control of the architect, the grand form of the cathedral or temple. His influence has been necessary to the highest triumph of their work and skill. So in that temple of the human soul, which each one of us is building, by the aid of so many noble faculties and graces, love is the architect. Love gives the lines for the foundation, and teaches all these diverse faculties how to work in their separate spheres, and how, thus working in their kind and nature, to subserve higher purposes by a Divine unity and moral excellence. Love gives value to all their work. Love unites their energies. Loves moves their faith and inspires their hope; and thus working together, they bring forth the temple of the living soul—greater than the temples of Greece; more enduring, more beautiful, more glorious than Solomon's temple; though, like his, built in silence: of noiseless thoughts, of voiceless affections, and of graces that have no noisy echo. "Now abideth faith, hope, charity, these three; but the greatest of these is charity." That destroys nothing worthy to be saved, but builds up all things in the soul; and, by giving to all and everything its place, gives to all and everything a nature and value and beauty better than they could ever have possessed, unless united and inspired by love.

When a man, then, is a Christian he dwells in love. Your growth in grace is not to be measured by your zeal in religious exercises, nor your glibness in prophecy, nor princely benefactions. These things may be well enough; but your growth in grace is in proportion to your love. He that dwelleth in love dwelleth in God.

THE PUZZLE OF THE POOR.

"THOU, O GOD, HAST PREPARED OF THY GOODNESS FOR THE POOR."—*Psalm lxviii. 10.*

How many the schemes that have been launched to get quit of poverty and its attendant evils! Each new nation and every century has had a panacea of its own. There have always been the poor with us, and there has always been the hope of getting quit of them—never stronger than during the last hundred years. Some of you know the words of a modern writer: "At the beginning of this marvellous era it was natural to expect, and it was expected, that labour-saving inventions would lighten the toil and improve the condition of the labourer; that the enormous increase in the power of producing wealth would make real poverty a thing of the past. Could a man of the last century—a Franklin or a Priestley—have seen in the vision of the future the steam-ship taking the place of the sailing vessel, the railroad train of the wagon, the reaping machine of the scythe; could he have heard the throb of the engines that exert a power greater than that of all the men and all the beasts of burden on the earth; could he have seen the forest tree transformed into finished lumber, into doors, sashes, blinds, boxes, and barrels, with hardly the touch of a human hand; the factories, where, under the eye of a girl, cloth is made faster than hundreds of stalwart weavers could have turned it out with their hand-looms; could he have seen steam hammers shaping mammoth shafts and mighty anchors, and delicate machinery making numberless watches; could he have realised the immense saving of labour resulting from improved facilities for exchange and communication; sheep killed in Australia, eaten fresh in Great Britain; the order given by the London banker executed in San Francisco in the morning of the same day—these and one hundred thousand improvements, what would he have inferred as to the social condition of mankind? Surely, that the bitter burden of poverty would now be swept away. It would not have seemed like an inference. It would have seemed as though he saw it; and his heart would have leaped, and his nerves would have thrilled, as one who from a height beholds, just ahead of the thirst-stricken caravan, the grateful green of fresh verdure and the gleam of laughing waters. He would have beheld these new forces elevating society from its foundations, lifting the very poorest above the possibility of want, and bringing in the golden age of which mankind have always dreamed. Youth no longer stunted and starved; age no longer harried by avarice; foul things fled; fierce things tame; discord turned to harmony." Then he goes on to lament that these have only been as dreams that men clutch at in the visions of the night. "Disappointment has followed disappointment. There has been discovery upon discovery, and invention upon invention; but they have neither lessened the toil of those who most need respite, nor brought plenty to the poor. From all parts of the civilised world come complaints of industrial depression, of labour massed and wasting, of pecuniary distress among business men, of want and suffering and anxiety among the working classes." Here, however, we would take issue with him. Bad as the condition of the poor may be, it is not worse, but better than it has been. Let us be thankful to God that, mainly through Christian virtue and Christian sacrifice, a forward march has been made all along the line. Its spirit of emancipation has put slavery to flight. Its spirit of wisdom has brought education within the reach of all; and its spirit of justice has extended wondrously political privilege and power. Ever since Christ was born in Bethlehem the world has been going uphill, not downhill. The bitter cry of poverty in our day is not half so bitter as it was in Greece and Rome. The soldiers that followed Bruce and Wallace to the battlefield came out from shelters little better than modern kennels; and one hundred and fifty years ago the colliers of Haddington were bought and sold with the estates. Even the lords of the ancient castles had not half the comforts of a modern room and kitchen. I have no sympathy with those who are always prating of the good old times, and disparaging those in which we live. I have read of the good old times of Queen Bess; and, at the same time, of lives consigned to the Tower on the most trivial causes; of venerable dames submitted to cruelty and torture as witches; and of labourers and their families subsisting upon what seems to us altogether insufficient.

In speaking of the puzzle of the poor, I am not referring to the class of vagrants that in my own day were wont to perambulate over the country—the gossipy beggar-wives and children that had their regular houses of call. They have been swept off by the Poor Law. Nor am I referring to the tramps who have taken their places — men, apparently workmen, who are always on the road between Newcastle and John o' Groat's House, looking for work—always unfortunate and always hungry. "Beg pardon, master; but could you spare us a copper to get something to eat?" This man lays himself pretty regularly at our gates full of sores, but he is not the Lazarus on whom we are to take pity. We ought to have labour houses to which they could apply, and then if they tramp and beg, we could take them up. Nor am I referring to that large class in our city that inhabit our model lodging-houses on the borders of tramp-dom, and sometimes over the border. They have no domestic ties, or they have ignored them; they have no ambition. They live by the way; take regular or odd jobs as they can get them, satisfied if they get as much as will pay for their food and their bed, and leave a margin for drink; or, rather, get sufficient for drink, and leave a margin for food. There is no puzzle about their lives. They are animalised. Lives, many of them begun brightly, that have somehow or another gone awry. There they are creeping to their couches, and still carrying within them the memories of homes filled with music. There has been within some of them heavenly aspirations, not yet altogether buried amid their besotted surroundings.

Nor am I at present dealing with the ninety-four thousand of the poor who have come under the care of the Parish Boards, as registered, casuals, or lunatics. Many of these belong essentially to the pauper class. Their parents failed in life, and fell under the care of the Parochial Board; and they went out a little bit into free life with their fellows and failed also, and came back upon the Board, either as residents within the house or for casual relief. The touch of the Poor Law is almost always fatal. I know a case where grandmother, mother, and grandchild—three generations—are getting relief from the Board. Then there are individual repeaters—one month in the house, one month in the world, one month in the house again, and so on, with an occasional visit to a convalescent home. And this I say with a thorough appreciation of the intelligence that is brought to bear on the Poor Law administration. It is a great puzzle how to deal with poverty so as to diminish it; to alleviate misery without creating paupers; and few people have any idea of the time and the talent given by our representatives. It is a matter for satisfaction that the tide is ebbing surely, if slowly. In 1869 the number of poor of all classes was 135,000, out of a population of 3⅓ million—about four per cent. Last year it was only 94,000, in a population of four millions—a percentage of little over two per cent. This puzzle might be much more easily solved, if people would only exercise a proper pride—nay, I might say, be true to their Christian principle, by assisting the poor of their own connection. It is in this sphere our true Lazarus lies. Some one, perhaps, who made our hearts glad when little boys or girls; or whose hands ministered to us in infancy and sickness; or the member of our circle who began to go down, and then for a long time appeared only at the funerals, as if to assert his common kinship, but who for many years has not been able to do that; or the child of that old friend whose face was as sunshine to your soul, to whose good counsel and good offices, possibly, we are indebted for much of our success. The Jews in London, in Glasgow, and in other places maintain their own poor. Why should not Christian families do it? My blood has boiled sometimes when a poor, shaky, old mother that had brought up half-a-dozen children, all in fair positions in the city, came to get me to sign the line by which she could take proceedings against them for support.

Who are the poor? The term is comparative. In California a man was reckoned poor that had not a homestead of his own—a house and lot free of debt; whereas, with this in a Scottish country village he would be numbered among the better classes.

I have been thinking a good deal about the puzzle life presents to those who, to use a homely expression, are not well off—who only by a struggle manage to attain the means of virtuous and honest life. I am thinking of the father who has to do the hard darg for 20s. or 25s. per week, and, in doing that, has to bear the slings and arrows of outrageous masters and gaffers; the thoughtful mother who lies down at night wondering when she will be able to get that new pair of boots for little Peter, who is delicate and needs them badly. I know her well. She has 25s. coming in (£65 per annum). There is a family of four, besides father and mother, to be fed, clothed, housed, heated, and educated. And this is a problem that has cost her a deal of thought. The rent is £9 18s.; taxes, £1 2s.; gas and water, £1 10s.; fuel, £3 10s.; tear and wear, £1 10s.; newspapers and literature, 10s.; clothing, £16; washing material, 10s.; society money and collections, £1; medical attendance, 12s.; church seat, 8s.; sundries, 10s.—£37; leaving £28, or 10s. 9d. per week, for food of all. It is on the mothers that this presses most, and it is amazing how they manage to do this. Some fail through their own inherent incapacity. Many are made to fail through causes over which they have no control—drinking, debt-getting, and sporting on the part of their partner. Others fail through causes which they themselves could help—a fondness for dressing above their station, and a readiness to get into debt. Drunkenness and debt are the great disturbing factors. I remember once, along with others, making a voyage in a canoe up one of our western rivers. It took us steady pulling to make way against the ordinary currents. It was hard work, but still very pleasant, to look away forward at the water sparkling in the sunlight, and around upon the stately pine trees—to see the deer as they came to quench their thirst at the brink, and to hear the wild duck and other water fowl as they flew from our disturbing presence. But in some portions of it we found the rapids, where the broken waters poured down with greater velocity and power. Through these we had to pull desperately and steer most carefully. By all exerting all our power we could just make way. If the prow veered but a little we were swept round and down. If any of us failed in our paddle stroke we were at once swept back, and had great difficulty in making up what we had lost. I have often thought that this is a fair picture of the position of many of our industrious poor. They have to pull all together to make way. It is a continuous struggle. If one member takes it easy, they cannot get forward. If one takes away by indulgence, it is hard to make it up again. If debt or drunkenness interfere, it is speedy failure. It must be a constant and steady pull all the time. But there are thousands of men and women in our city who thus maintain a respectable and virtuous life. They are the strength and glory of our country. They patiently toil on with a great courage, happy if their labour makes them independent; only disposed to complain when work is wanting. And they are keenly alive to all means of improvement; have a most intelligent interest in all the questions of the day, and keen sympathy with the moral progress of the period. They are the members of our Intellectual Societies, Assurance Societies, Oddfellows' Societies, Shepherds' and Gardeners' Unions, and of our Christian Churches. I don't want to disparage any class; but by far the most interested members in the Church and its varied schemes have come from this very class. Look at those churches where such people form the bulk of the membership. They are model churches in zeal, in liberality, and in kindness to the minister.

I don't know how they manage to work out this puzzle of life. Christian principle has a great deal to do with it. These people are made earnest by the very difficulties with which they have to deal. They seek the wisdom that cometh down from above; they meditate much; they look along the lines, and think of the future for themselves and their children; they tremble for them amid the temptations of life. They know that their children will have to go out and work alongside of some that are coarse and unprincipled, and hear filthy talk, and learn about things to which they have been strangers. And so while they teach, they also pray for their children. They have not forgotten the injunction, "Cast thy burden upon the Lord, and He shall sustain thee."

We have read many books proposing to deal with the problems that press upon the masses. Some of those schemes may be helpful, and some are not. They all proceed upon the theory that if somehow, by giving people an interest in the land, or more control of the government, or binding all into a great social union, or in any other way producing a perfect set of circumstances outside, then they will get men and women and children peaceful, prosperous, and happy. This is well enough in its way. In better outside circumstances there may be more encouragement to thrift and to virtue; but, after all, it is not in our stars, but in ourselves that we are underlings. One ounce of principle in the heart is worth more than hundredweights of political economy in the world beyond. If a man has the spirit of Christ, the spirit of hardy virtue, the spirit of self-sacrifice, the love of that which is pure and honest, his lack of wealth and ease will be no great evil. All things are his; his to walk erect with independent mind; his the joy of the strife and the joy of victory; his the reward of his Lord, who triumphed gloriously amid poverty, persecution, and death. We speak of those who are well born; and too often we think of those who are born of rank, of honourable name, and of wealth. To be well born is to be born of health, to be born of habits trained to industry, to be born of piety. Thomas Carlyle was well born, though his father was a hard working stonemason; his friend Edward Irving was well born, though his mother was a widow almost from the time of his birth; and David Livingstone was well born; and hundreds of others, who have felt the touch of poortith and learned to bear the yoke in their youth. "Blessed is the man that walketh not in the counsel of the ungodly, nor standeth in the way of sinners, nor sitteth in the seat of the scornful: but his delight is in the law of the Lord; and in His law doth he meditate day and night."

THE PUZZLE OF THE RICH.

"CHARGE THEM THAT ARE RICH IN THIS WORLD, THAT THEY BE NOT HIGH-MINDED, NOR TRUST IN UNCERTAIN RICHES, BUT IN THE LIVING GOD, WHO GIVETH US RICHLY ALL THINGS TO ENJOY."—*1 Timothy vi. 17.*

GOETHE, the great German, who, like our own Shakespeare, knew almost everything, said: "Everything in the world may be endured, except only a succession of prosperity." This does not seem true at first sight. We have spoken of the great struggle presented to the heads of many a virtuous household in bringing up a family of six on 24s. or 25s. a week; and it looks at first sight as if all this anxiety and toil could be removed by pouring in among the working classes the affluent streams of wealth; and yet, when we more fully consider the matter, there is as much anxiety and far more danger in having £6,000 a year than in having £60.

We are all creatures of limited capacity. Mere wealth cannot enlarge our capacity; cannot protect us against the disappointments of life; cannot ensure freedom from the ailments of life; and cannot buy off death. However large his estate, the rich man cannot get out of it more than his food and his clothing. It has been said that he can secure more pleasures. Even this is doubtful, for the simple and natural pleasures of the poor are sweeter, more enduring, and safer. The rich man is only a trustee. He must dispense it himself; or, if he hoards up wealth, he must leave it to be scattered by others.

The first part of the puzzle is this:—How to hold wealth so as not to be the worse of it in the individual or in the family.

When I came to Glasgow I was present at a large assembly held in the City Hall. I was a stranger. I did not know many of the people present; but there sat beside me a beautiful boy of about eleven or twelve years of age. He told me the names of all the people, and showed me every attention. I asked his name. He was the son of one of our foremost men, who, the son of a widow, had begun life near the High Street, and had to labour hard in earlier days. He had prospered; and now his son had good education, good manners, good connection, a good home, and the prospect of starting life with wealth and position. I pictured to myself the bright career of that lad. I argued—If his father has risen in our city from the poor starting point, to how much higher position must he rise from a better starting point? The richness of that home proved to be no advantage. He was amiable, but he was soft. He went forth into the lists of life, and he fell. He entered his father's warehouse, but he learned little there. He could not do the work half so well as the sons of shoemakers, tinkers, and tailors round about him. They could be relied on, but he could not. Then there came the whisper of shady things; then followed disgrace and degradation. Death overtook him when he had scarcely turned thirty-one. This case has led me many a time to deplore the effect of wealth upon hundreds. In many homes there is usually too much food, too much company, too many solicitations to pleasure, too frequent absence on the part of parents, and too little care of the companionship of the children. Good companions for our children are not those that have wealth and fine homes. I should say, from personal experience, that the children of shepherds and small farmers are the best companions. Sir Walter Scott found it so. The result too often is softness in boyhood, irreverence in youth, instability in manhood, and ruin ere age is reached.

I have seen some strange imitations in my time. Among others, I have known a collier, by his perseverance and good judgment, come to have more than three million pounds, and, what says more for him, spent it wisely in great public works, in building railways through hitherto pathless forests, and such like. He was born in a "but and a ben" near Kilmarnock, and he died leaving a big castle and a great fortune to his children. Will they do as well? Even he would have been a better man had he been less successful. I regard with distrust the influence of wealth upon individuals. It may be used, it has been used, for good to others; but I more than doubt whether the chances lean that way. Leisure and luxury are almost always bad for every man. I have seen so much of the evil of wealth upon the mind, making it proud and haughty and impatient; robbing it of its simplicity, modesty, and humility; drying up within it the fountains of gentleness and generosity; and I have heard so much from others, that I more and more distrust its boasted advantages. Some of the richest men have been the very poorest. With big estates and big accounts, they were essentially small men. Almost all the noblest things that have been achieved in the world have been achieved by poor men—poor scholars and professional men, poor artisans and artists, poor philosophers and poets, and men of genius and invention. James Watt perfected his engine when on the verge of bankruptcy. Burns published his poems to try and get £20; and Charles Dickens learned much of philosophy and of the world when ministering to his father in a prison. It is good for us to bear the yoke, and especially to bear the yoke in our youth. Many children are injured by too much attention, too many servants at home, too many lessons at school, too many indulgences in society. They are taken out of the school of Providence and placed in one which wealth and a foolish pride have built for them. Where there is wealth it would be often better to board out the children with poor people on the distant moor. No small part of the puzzle to the rich is to keep this taint of wealth and luxury from affecting the character of their children.

Nor does the peril attach to individuals and families alone, but to cities and to empires. The lessons of past history are solemnly emphatic. The history of wealth has always been a history of corruption and downfall. People can never long stand the trial. "Everything in the world may be endured, except only a succession of prosperity."

The second part of the puzzle is in the keeping of riches. They make themselves wings and fly away.

When, a few years ago, the estates of a Scottish nobleman were sold and divided out among successful quarrymen and others, I said to one of our leading manufacturers: "Why has the earl been obliged to sell his lands? He is a man of pure life, and has no extravagant habits." "Why," he said, "it is as difficult to *keep* wealth as to *make* it." In my boyhood there was an old estate which belonged to a baronet of honourable lineage. There was a boy, born and brought up in a gardener's house, not far from his gate, who used to take a ramble through his woods, and who was frequently chased from them by the keepers. The heir of the baronet gradually lost. That boy entered a factory and gradually gained. That fine old estate passed, some years ago, from the heir to the gardener's lad. Years ago, in paying the premium on my insurance, a large property-holder met me, and said, "Insurance is a poor investment. I can do better with money." I replied, and the sequel proved that my reply had some influence. Some years after he failed, notwithstanding the boasted power of investing. The surrender value of the policy of his life, about £40, and £100 received for his furniture, were the only assets against thousands of debt. Verily, it is as difficult to hold wealth, whether in land or capital, as to gather wealth. The gentry-houses of Glasgow have changed hands again and again.

The third part of the puzzle is how to spend money. There are some who try to solve it by not giving at all, but the grip must slacken some time; they are merely leaving it for others.

There is, at the mouth of the Mississippi in the sea, a huge delta—an accumulation of mud brought down through many ages, filled with fertilising matter; and there is on its banks, not far away, barren stretches of sand and weeds. There is as much in that mass of mud as would cover all this barren territory, and cause it to bring forth the precious fruit. The mud is massed in the wrong place; while other places are sterile without it. The difficulty is to get it transferred to the parts where it is needed. This is the difficulty presented by the massing of wealth among some classes, and the poverty that reigns among others. It is said that there is enough in the world for all; nay, it is admitted that there is also sufficient charity in the hearts of men to draw forth that abundance to supply the need of all. But there is a doubt which charitable persons continually have as to whether they are doing good or the reverse. This picture has been given: "A wearied workman, returning home from his work on a winter evening, sees through the window of some house a blazing fire, a cosy room, and the family seated at a well-covered table, surrounded by every comfort; while he is going to a cheerless home, where there will hardly be coal enough to cook his supper." If the head of that family had been looking out at the window when the poor man was looking in, probably the prompting of his heart would be to go out and give him of his abundance; or he might refrain, and say, "I have no right to interfere with his sturdy self-reliance, nor interfere with the great law of industry and compensation;" but he would return feeling as if he had no right to enjoy his meal with such poverty at his door. And he might have been right in giving. There might have been special circumstances in the house of that man that would have made the friendly aid at the time a real blessing—a seasonable help that would have been a grateful remembrance all his life. But he might also have been right in refusing. There might have been no special occasion; and the gift might have stirred up the thought, "If I can get so much so easily, why should I not try again? Or if the gentleman is so good and so rich, why should I not make a personal appeal to him?" And thus there would have been begun all that is servile and mean, in one man slothfully sucking his substance from another. It is a duty, a joy, and a privilege to help those who are doing all they can to help themselves; but it is *wrong* to help those who are disposed to lean upon us. The following is related as an apt illustration by Mr. Polson, of Paisley, who has looked at this: A man died, and left his fortune—£20,000—to be equally divided between his two sons. They both recognised the duty of being faithful stewards, but they took different ways of acquitting themselves of that duty. One set aside a portion of his inheritance to be distributed as a charity, so that he might with a good conscience settle down and enjoy the rest. With this portion he made a gift to every family in the village where he resided. The other invested his £10,000 in a spinning factory. Ten years afterwards the results were noted, and they stood thus: Of the gifts of money no trace remained, except here and there a worn-out bonnet or shawl, or some little article of furniture. And there was a long list of bad results on the other side, such as, that the head of the household, when he got money into his hand, put his hat on his head, and went out to enjoy himself, and had never done any good afterwards. The balance was very much on the wrong side. In regard to the other—the mill had given regular employment to a large number of poor people during all these years, fostered habits of industry and regularity, and diffused happiness and comfort through the whole village. Besides, the enterprise had been successful. The £10,000 had become £20,000, the mill had doubled in size, the village increased; and the owner, working in the Divinely appointed lines of action, had made his inheritance a blessing to himself and all around. He did this with the intelligent, deliberate intention of benevolence; but even if he had been seeking his own increase, still the use of his capital, in accordance with God's law, would have done good.

An Ayrshire lad came to Glasgow and gathered a fortune. By nature kindly and benevolent, he gave away money every day to objects he approved of, and sometimes to objects he did not much approve of. As the day drew near when he must lay down earthly toil, he often thought about what should be done with the money he had made. He spoke about it. One day he said, "What would you do if you had as much money as I have?" "Build an East-End infirmary," I replied. "Well," he said, "I have thought of that;" and went on to discuss that and other things. He hesitated, and death overtook him.

These, then, are the serious puzzles of the rich—How to have wealth, and not be the worse of it in the individual or in the family; and how to distribute it so as to do good, and not evil. The second is a commercial question, which I cannot discuss fully. All that I will say is, that the fear of God, and obedience to His holy and good law, goes a long way to the keeping of wealth, as well as health. Dissipation, wild speculation, and extravagance go a long way to the destruction of wealth. As one said to me: "The young laird was a fine fellow; he was a finer fellow than the old laird; but he was fond of racing, and he put his money on the horses, and they started and they ran—away with his money."

In regard to the puzzle of having wealth in such a way as not to be the worse of it in the individual or in the family, men must hold it in the spirit of stewardship. If they would think: "This has come to me not for my own selfish purposes, but for God and for the world." They must spend, but in all spending manifest principle. The wealthy must take up the lesson of the Cross and *deny* themselves; then teach their children to do the same. This is the highest style of life, and it is safest for them and for their's. As the man who is on the verge of the fatal current, which has swept others away, clings all the more tenaciously to the rocks by its side, so ought men of wealth, almost desperately, to hold on to the life of simplicity and self-denial as it is in Christ Jesus.

How will the rich give so as not to hurt, but to benefit? Give always according to their knowledge, or through responsible bodies that they approve of. We are too ready to seek grand far-off schemes, and not willing to help those that are near and known to us. Giving is not sufficiently personal. People could do a great deal of good among their own relatives. The rich and poor are strangely bound together. Men and women go forth from the same family circle to such different fates. Then, again, rich people could do much to follow out the example of the early Church in caring for its poor. On the verge of every congregation there are many to whom good can be judiciously done. There is too little of this feeling. People say, "We pay the seat rent." That is a mere outside relationship, not a Christian relationship. I always attempt to get a poor family put in relationship to one better off. The personal touch and sympathy is of great value to both; but some resent this almost rudely. They say, "What are these to me?" "I have enough to do with my own." They ignore the spirit of Christ, and do not consider the good effect this might have upon their families. It would save them often from the selfishness they deplore.

The great matter is to "follow after charity" with knowledge and a good conscience. The spirit of Christ brings rich and poor together in a right way. It teaches both, not to be exacting, but to be considerate of each other, and to sympathise with each other's difficulties. Perhaps the most beautiful experiments of modern days are those of Toynbee Hall. There we behold the sons of the rich and the noble dwelling in the midst of the poor, in order, by personal knowledge and effort, to alleviate their woes and exalt their condition. Nothing more chivalrous has been recorded in history. Charity and knowledge must go together.

The rich man's son inherits lands,
    And piles of brick and stone and gold,
And he inherits soft white hands,
    And tender flesh that fears the cold ;
    Nor does he wear a garment old.
A heritage, it seems to me,
One scarce would care to hold in fee.

What doth the poor man's son inherit ?
    Stout muscles and a sinewy heart,
A hardy frame, a hardier spirit ;
    King of two hands, he does his part
    In every useful toil and art.
A heritage, it seems to me,
 A king might wish to hold in fee.

Oh ! rich man's son, there is a toil
    That with all other level stands ;
Large charity doth never soil,
    But only soften white soft hands.
    This is the best crop for thy lands.
A heritage, it seems to me,
Worth being rich to hold in fee.

Oh ! poor man's son, scorn not thy state ;
    There is worse weariness than thine,
In merely being rich or great.
    Toil only gives the soul to shine,
    And makes rest fragrant and Divine.
A heritage, it seems to me,
Worth being poor to hold in fee.

Both heirs to some six feet of sod,
    Are equal in the earth at last ;
Both children of the same dear God,
    Prove title to your heirship vast,
    By records of a well-filled past.
A heritage, it seems to me,
Well worth a life to hold in fee.

A FOOLISH KING.

I KINGS XII.

We behold the Israelites at an interesting period of their national history. A hereditary monarchy had been instituted, but not firmly fixed. There was still some danger of defection, and that defection was hastened by the foolishness of the son of Solomon. "Strange!" says an old writer, "that though Solomon had a thousand wives, yet we read but of one son that he had to bear up his name, and that son was a fool." Thus, neither wisdom nor wit run in the blood. Not all the learning of Athens could redeem the son of Cicero from idiocy; not all the power of Cromwell could establish the government of Britain for his son; not all the grace of Chesterfield could make a fine gentleman of his son; nor could all the wisdom of Solomon save his son from folly. Although he had been the darling of a Court where the wise and the learned gathered together, yet no sooner did he grasp the reins of power than he signalized himself by imprudence, obstinacy, and cruelty. There seems to have been some premonition of this in the mind of the aged Solomon. As he looked back upon the progress of his kingdom, and forward to its probable fate, he gave vent to his feelings in that doleful prophecy: "I hated all my labour which I had taken under the sun, because I should leave it to the man which shall be after me, and who knoweth whether he shall be a wise man or a fool. Yet shall he rule over my labour wherein I have laboured and shewed myself wise under the sun."

We see that the sovereignty of David's house was yet new and unsettled. For, observe that, instead of all the people coming up to Jerusalem to congratulate their new king, Rehoboam goes down to Shechem to seek their confirmation of his right.

The country appears to have been in the condition of England previous to the Norman Conquest. From the time of Egbert, in 800, our monarchy was hereditary; yet, on the succession of every new king, the Witenagemote, or grand council of the nation, met to confirm the title by a formal election.

The pretence of this assembly at Shechem was to make Rehoboam king, but the real purpose was to unmake him. There was already the lurking spirit of revolution. Both the place and the spokesman manifest this. Shechem! why, the very place was associated with treachery. At Shechem was Joseph sold by his brethren; at Shechem did Gad rally his followers against Abimelech; at Shechem did Abimelech raise his treacherous standard against his brethren. It could not fail to put Israel in mind of rebellion; the very soil was stained by perfidiousness. The spokesman was Jeroboam, the very man that had plotted conspiracy in the days of Solomon and had fled to Egypt. A fugitive from his country, he had long lurked in a foreign Court, and now he embraces the occasion of Solomon's death to return. Crafty and unprincipled, he fires the smouldering spirit of revolution. It says little for their allegiance to the memory of Solomon that they were so ready to receive him. It was bad to entertain a rebel; it was worse to countenance him; and worst of all to employ him. Many a people in those rough times would have presented his head to their new king, instead of letting him go as their head.

The speech is no better than the speech-maker. In one

hand he holds a petition, and in the other a sword. All the time he is making professions of servility he is seeking the occasion of defiance. "Thy father made our yoke grievous." It had been the boast of the early part of Solomon's reign that no Israelites—only foreigners—were employed in compulsory labour. But that had passed away, and Solomon, like other Oriental despots, had assumed the absolute right to such services from his subjects as he needed from them, and had classified them, and appointed officers over them for this purpose. This was a real grievance, but not their greatest. "Thy father made our yoke grievous." This is the chief burden of their complaint. They complain, but observe not one word in regard to Solomon's idolatry and revolt from God. That which was really the greatest grievance is none to them. Oh, Israel, Israel, how hast thou fallen? They are anxious about their own interest, but indifferent in regard to far higher interests. God or Moloch—it was all one whom they might worship, so that they could live at ease and pay no taxes.

We turn now to the conduct of Rehoboam. His first resolution becomes the son of Solomon. He asks time for consideration. "Depart yet for three days, then come again to me." He who had shown so much wisdom in calling for leisure showed but little wisdom in the improvement of that leisure. The aged friends of his father are first summoned to his council. "What counsel give ye me to return answer to this people?" It seems as if something corresponding to the modern idea of a responsible ministry had prevailed in the days of Solomon, for these men are designated as the old men that had stood before Solomon his father while he yet lived. It had been their practice to give advice in regard to the affairs of the former kingdom during the former reign, and they came most willingly to the assistance of the young king. "How do ye advise that I may answer this people?" Unanimously they reply: "If thou wilt be a servant unto this people this day, and wilt serve them, and answer them, and speak good words unto them, then they will be thy servants for ever." "What a beautiful address! What good advice!" How different from the speeches made in these days to Oriental tyrants! "If thou wilt be the servant of this people." How delicately they remind him of the duty of his high position and the relation he sustains to his subjects. All serve the king, but the true king serves all. No false men these, inflating his youthful mind with ideas of Divine Right and thoughts of tyranny. Happy had it been for the nations if these words had been inscribed on every palace of the world: "Speak good words unto them." Good words are worth much and cost little. Haughtiness repels; urbanity attracts. A rude address bruises no muscles, but it hurts all the same. "Hard words break no bones," says the proverb. No, they do not break bones, but they *break hearts*; and, brethren, I beseech you, whether you have to deal with subordinates in your daily labours, or with the members of your family, or the dependents within your homes, remember the advice of these aged counsellors—"Speak good words unto them." But they continued: "Then will they be thy servants for ever." It is so easy for men in high position to gain favour. Dignified kindness would have shamed the people out of their conceit with Jeroboam. His true royalty would have contrasted favourably with the pretentious renegade. By stooping he might have conquered.

There is one thing better than even the ability to give good advice, and that is the willingness to take good advice. This Rehoboam was unwilling to do. If the people were credulous and covetous, he was rash and impetuous. Was he to be dictated to by a parcel of rebels? Could men in their dotage be suitable advisers for the heir to the throne of Solomon? Good enough measures these for the days gone by, but more energetic measures now for the new era inaugurated. In the multitude of counsellors there is wisdom. "I will apply to the men of my own day—to the companions of my leisure hours before I was king." Such were his thoughts, and so we read: "He forsook the counsel of the old men, and consulted with the young men who were brought up with him." In order that we may judge how unfit these men were to give advice we must remember that it was the custom of Oriental kings to keep the heirs presumptive to the throne confined within the palace or the seraglio, lest factions should form around them; and companions were allotted to them, whose accomplishments were of the kind to amuse rather than to be useful. This so far explains the imbecility of Rehoboam, and his utter ignorance of public affairs. It also explains the incapacity of those who had been brought up with him to advise in matters pertaining to the weal of the kingdom. Their only duty had been to amuse, to flatter, to sing songs and play instruments. Theirs were frivolities of the chamber rather than the virtues of the statesman or legislator. Nay, all great and good men are always held in contempt by such insolent and insignificant flatterers; and these were the men to whom, unfortunately, the young king turned in this crisis. When the Duke of Sully was called upon by Louis XIII. to give his advice in some great emergency, he observed the favourites of the Court whispering together at his unfashionable appearance. "Whenever your Majesty's father," said the old warrior and statesman, "did me the honour to consult me, he ordered the buffoons of the Court to retire into the ante-chamber." Better had it been for Rehoboam had he kept these for the chamber rather than the Court; for the *light-minded* are *foolhardy*. They do not realise responsibility. Their thought was all of royal rights and prerogatives, not of royal duties. Scorning to be braved by the base vulgar, they put words of assumed greatness upon the tongue of their prince, that he may teach these subordinates to know their master. " My little finger shall be thicker than my father's loins. My father chastised you with whips, I will chastise you with scorpions "— that is to say, that whereas his father had scourged them with simple whips, he would scourge them with twisted lashes armed with sharp and lacerating points—for to such the name of scorpion was given. Their answer has the colour of courage, but it is really the result of weakness. Courage is the daughter of prudence; rashness the off-spring of folly and presumption. Courage considers all the circumstances of danger, and faces them; rashness is blind to all danger, and leaps boldly, only to hide inherent timidity.

On the third day the young king again stands before his expectant people. Jeroboam had been active, meanwhile, among them, sowing the seeds of discontent; yet Rehoboam falters not. As we read, he forsook the counsel of the old men, and answered them roughly. He speaks the speech as it was spoken to him by the young men; and why, the very words have stings. The message cannot but provoke. Ah! they think, if he can thus draw blood with his tongue, how much more with his hands! If he speak thus at the beginning of his reign, what will he do at the end of it? What a terrible instrument of mischief is the tongue. A good tongue is the trumpet of God; a bad tongue is the firebrand of hell. Well did the old philosophers, when asked what was the best member of the body, reply—"The tongue;"

and when asked what was the worst—" The tongue."
Therewith bless we God. Therewith curse we man. That
short speech of Rehoboam did more than a thousand
others could undo. It roused the people already disaffected
to open rebellion. In the violence of their fury they not
only turned against Rehoboam, but against the house of
David. " To your tents, O Israel! see to thine own house, O
David!" was the cry that arose all around. And although
no words of upbraiding were returned, and no blow struck,
a rupture had taken place that was never healed. Of the
twelve tribes of Israel only two—Judah and Benjamin—
remained faithful. The other ten retired to establish a
separate kingdom. So suddenly and quietly had all hap-
pened that the king could scarce believe the revolt was real
or general. He remained at Shechem—in the very heart of
the disaffected districts, and might have remained longer,
had it not been for his infatuated obstinacy. He took it
into his head to set the most obnoxious person in the land
—one Adoram, the head tax-gatherer—to collect, on the
very spot, the burdensome taxes which had caused the complaint. This was too much for the Shechemites. They
stoned Adoram to death. This opened the king's eyes, and,
mounting his chariot, he drove in hot haste to Jerusalem,
nor paused till he was once more within its citadel; a king,
indeed, but denuded of the greater portion of his possessions; and the end of his days was surrounded with anarchy,
foreign war, and disaster.

Let me apply this—first, in a particular way; second, in
a general way.

Rehoboam's father had prepared a book for his special instruction—the Book of Proverbs. If ever he looked over that
book in the midst of his troubled life, how sadly must his eye
have lingered on that sentence: " He that walketh with wise

men shall be wise, but the companion of fools shall be destroyed!" How often, in later days, when he contemplated the small proportions of his territory, and saw even the temple of the Lord stripped of its riches by the Egyptian king—how often would he dolefully recall those words: "The companion of fools shall be destroyed;" and how often since has the history of princes borne testimony to its truth—"The companion of fools shall be destroyed!" Nay, by experience, in every rank and condition of life, it is continually re-echoed—"The companion of fools shall be destroyed." To many a lowly home, as to many a lordly mansion, has this sad truth penetrated with bitter, bitter anguish and despair—"The companion of fools shall be destroyed." The choosing of his company is as much a matter of transcendent importance to the peasant as to the prince. Young man! young woman! I implore you to remember—"The companion of fools shall be destroyed."

Second, generally.—We cannot fail to perceive how the prosperity of nations is largely dependent on their rulers. Rehoboam was foolish, and Israel was divided. The two parts harassed and weakened each other, as Scotland and England used to do, and both became, in turn, the victims of Syria, Assyria, and Babylon. We may trace the captivity in Babylon to the folly of Rehoboam. History is full of such examples. The wise councils of Elizabeth gave birth to a strength, prosperity. and enterprise, which the folly of the Stuarts could not wholly subvert. The prosperity and the purity of our own day have been promoted by the virtues, the motherly and womanly qualities, of a Victoria, and by the concealed wisdom of Albert the Good; whereas, under misrule, Greece, the original home of poetry, eloquence, and philosophy, was for many centuries dead and degraded.

THE TEMPLE OF SOLOMON.

"Thus all the work that Solomon made for the house of the Lord was finished."—*1 Kings vii. 51.*

(Preached, when Grand Chaplain of Scotland, to the Masonic Lodge in Cathedral, Glasgow.)

There are four edifices mentioned in Scripture in connection with the worship of the Jews. The Tabernacle built in the wilderness, carried on their marches into the Promised Land, and finally set up in Jerusalem. There are three Temples—the Temple built by Solomon, 1,000 years before Christ; the Temple built by Zerubbabel, 560 years before Christ; and the Temple built by Herod shortly before the birth of Christ. The first Temple was twice the size of the Tabernacle, which was thirty cubits long, ten cubits high, and ten cubits broad. The Temple was thus not so very large, but very rich in its adorning, and with great courts round about it. The second Temple was twice the size of the first, and the Temple of Herod grander and more beautiful than those that preceded.

When King David had overcome his enemies, and found a period of rest, his thoughts reverted to the care of God's House. The Tabernacle had long served as the visible dwelling-place of Jehovah. But David was not content with this. It might be good enough for the tribes, when travelling, but not for the people established in the land; and so one day he expressed these thoughts to Nathan, the friend and counsellor: "Lo, I dwell in a house of cedars, but the Ark of the Lord God remaineth under curtains." Then Nathan said to David: "Do all that is in thine heart, for God is with thee." And it came to pass the same night that the word of the Lord came to Nathan. "Go and tell David, my servant, saying: 'Thou shalt not build Me an house to dwell in. Thy son, which shall be after thee, he shall build me an house.'" This was a great disappointment—as great to David as the announcement was to Moses, that after guiding the Children of Israel to the very borders of the Promised Land, he was not to enter in. His heart was set upon the work. God had poured into his soul rich streams of song, and he longed to give these a place in exalted ritual. But like a strong man, he bent himself to the blow. He could not enter upon the work, but he could collect treasure and material for it. Nay, he could prepare the plan for it. It was ever before him. Thus he addressed Solomon, in the presence of all the princes and captains:— "Be strong, and of good courage, and do it. Fear not, nor be dismayed; for the Lord God, even my God, will be with thee. He will not fail thee nor forsake thee."

David fell asleep in a good old age, and Solomon was called to reign in his stead. Peace and prosperity signalized the opening years of his reign. Israel, from being a warlike province, came to be a great commercial nation. His allies came from afar. In a short period, his sway extended over the whole territory between the Nile and the Euphrates. Among others, Hiram, king of Tyre, distinguished himself. He supplied him with men and materials—"timber of fir, timber of cedar, and algum trees." Four years were spent in preparation and seven in the work itself. All the stones were hewn in their far-off quarries, and all the beams and other pieces of wood-work shaped at a distance. The foundation of it had to be prepared on Mount Moriah, the spot where Abraham of old set himself to offer up Isaac. It was a high, abrupt hill, with a narrow summit, and it required immense containing walls to be built up from the valley beneath, to enlarge its summit, so as to give space for the Temple. These were of the most substantial nature, and have endured to the present day. Then the building of the Temple proceeded in silence No sound of hammer or axe was heard. The work was entrusted to Hiram, a skilled architect; and there were employed 3,000 overseers and 30,000 Israelites in Lebanon; also, 70,000 Canaanites carrying burdens, and 80,000 cutting stones out in the quarries. For labour so great and so long continued, it was comparatively small. Many of our modern temples are much larger. It was only about 90 feet long, 30 feet high, and 30 feet broad—the Porch in front four times higher. It was not in size, but in the richness of its material and workmanship that it excelled. When we remember that this was built of white marble on the steep front of a hill, we can easily conceive the impressive appearance it presented. The whole of the interior corresponded to the wealth and beauty of the exterior. Its inner walls, beams, posts, doors, floors, and ceilings, were made of olive and cedar wood, covered with plates of gold, and adorned with jewels. The very nails which fastened the plates were of gold, with heads of curious workmanship. The roof was of olive wood, covered with gold; and when the sun shone thereon, the reflection was of such refulgent splendour that it dazzled the eyes of all that beheld it. All the vessels used in the sacrifice were suited to the richness of the edifice.

For seven long years did the structure slowly rise before the eyes of the inhabitants. At length the work was completed, and the copestone brought forth with shoutings. It was a solemn yet joyous day in Jerusalem. The multitude of people thronged the courts and stretched away down the streets to the very walls of the city. Attracting every eye, crowning the summit of Mount Moriah, stood the Temple, with its lofty columns, and great tower, and gilded roof sparkling in the sunlight of heaven—the visible dwelling-place of Jehovah, the joy of the whole earth, and the symbol of that other, not made with hands, eternal in the heavens. Solomon himself dedicated the Temple to the Most High, in that prayer recorded in the sixth chapter of 2nd Chronicles. "But will God indeed dwell with men on earth? Behold, heaven and the heaven of heavens cannot contain Thee: how much less this house which I have built! Have respect, therefore, unto the prayer of Thy servant, and to his supplication, O Lord, my God! to hearken unto the prayer which Thy servant prayeth before Thee." Most impressive must have been the sight of the young king, in his royal robes, thus officiating, while the thousands of Levites and priests within sounded their trumpets, and raised the great chorus: "Praise the Lord, for He is good: for His mercy endureth for ever."

The Temple and its furniture not only served the purposes of worship for the people, who were bound, at least three times a year, to go up to it, but they were symbolic of spiritual things beyond, and typical of the future. Rich in itself and its instruments, it was richer still in the associations with which its existence was bound up.

In it there were three parts—the Porch, the Holy Place, the Holy of Holies. The Porch stood between the outer world and the Holy Place, where was the brazen candlestick—darkness on the outside, light within. This represents the soul turning away from the world and darkness, and seeking the fellowship of the blessed ones. There is the light of the Word, and of ordinances—light, but not perfect light, yet leading on to that which is beyond. Beyond the Holy Place there was the Most Holy Place. There was the Ark, and the Mercy-Seat, and the Shechinah, the visible light of the Eternal. Into this the High Priest entered only once a year, having made a sacrifice for himself and his order. There was thus symbolized the Great High Priest who came to render Himself a sacrifice for sin, and also the heaven into which He has entered to make intercession for His people. It set forth that Holy of Holies where God Himself is the light, and into whose presence there can in no wise enter anything that defileth, neither whatsoever worketh abomination or maketh a lie, but they which are written in the Lamb's book of life. There, when the work is done and the warfare accomplished, is the worker to be received and owned before angels and holy spirits. "Come, ye blessed of My Father; enter into the joy of thy Lord."

The Temple spoke to the Israelites of present privilege and of future hope. It was the type and prophecy of the Mighty One who was to come—CHRIST, THE LORD. Through Him we enter into higher privileges, closer communion with God, and a clearer hope. "Beloved, now are we the sons of God; and it doth not yet appear what we shall be: but we know that, when He shall appear, we shall be like Him; for we shall see Him as He is." We shall see Him as He is. Even by the best lights here we see Him but dimly and afar off. We do not fully understand Him, but then we shall see Him and be like Him. In but a little time there we shall have made degrees in knowledge and in virtue, compared with which, all that we learned here is but a trifle.

A practical lesson is for ever taught in the building of this Temple—*thoroughness*. All the material was of the richest quality, and all the workmanship of the most careful character. Even the stones of the foundation, hidden out of sight, were not ragged and rude, but hewn and costly; and the ornaments away up in the obscurest parts perfect of their kind. God's eye is over all. The Great Master is to be served by true and faithful work. We can glorify Him in obscure as well as in conspicuous positions. Every stone in its own course. Every man in his own order, whether high or low. We are to be true and genuine in work as well as word.

That grand Temple was built in silence; the materials were brought from afar. And so in silence do we build up the temple of our spiritual being. We gather the materials from every quarter—from every word we hear, every book we read, every transaction in which we have a part. What shall the Temple be—fair and beautiful, filled with grace, or flimsy and worthless, only to be rejected for ever?

> So build we up the being that we are:
> Thus deeply drinking in the soul of things,
> We shall be wise perforce.
>   Whate'er we see,
> Whate'er we feel, by agency direct
> Or indirect, shall tend to feed and nurse
> Our faculties; shall fix in calmer seats
> Of moral strength, and raise to loftier heights
> Of love divine, our intellectual soul.

"In My Father's house are many mansions." I daresay you know the old tradition by which St. John was called the Architect in the early days. And why? One of the early saints had a dream of heaven. He was admitted within the gates of pearl, to walk along the golden streets, and he gazed upon the many mansions of the Father's house. Looking upon some that were even more beautiful than others, he asked how they had been built. "Ah!" said the angel-guide, "these are the works of St. John. For every good deed done, for every good word spoken, by the saints down yonder, the angels add a course to the mansion that is a-building here for that saint. And these are the works of St. John. He has been a great architect." Remember that whatever the gear we may gather, whatever the houses we may erect, or whatever the lands we may acquire, the only thing we can take away into that other world is the Temple of our Character.

THE ELECT LADY.

2 JOHN I. I.

(Lecture in Blackfriars, 23rd April, 1893.)

THOMAS FULLER—that quaintest of the olden writers—says, "To describe a holy state without a virtuous lady therein were to paint a year without a spring." The Bible contains many narratives of the piety and faith of woman. If first in transgression, she has ever been the first in works of faith and labours of love. Woman illustrates every page of history by her courage, her affection, and her patience. The one sweet resting-place in the pilgrimage of Christ was the home in Bethany. There the *Man* Christ Jesus stands in softened majesty and tenderness before our view. We there see Martha—bustling, energetic, impulsive, grappling with the stern realities and routine of life; and there we see Mary—calm, meek, devotional, ill suited to battle with the cares and sorrows of a rough world. As it has been said, "Martha was one of those meteor spirits, rushing to and fro amid the ceaseless activities of life, softened and saddened, but not crushed, by the inroads of sorrow. Mary, again, we think of as one of those angel forms which now and then seem to walk the earth from the spirit land—a quiet evening star, shedding its mellowed radiance among deepening twilight shadows as if her home was in a brighter sphere, and her choice that better part which could not be taken from her."

Christianity has raised the position of woman; and woman, in return, has been the brightest ornament of Christianity.

One of the best arguments for the truth, as it is in Christ, is the illustration which it has received in the lives and labours of numberless Christian women. The memory of a mother has been the saving cause in the history of many a man whose steps were tiding on to evil and danger. We can never forget how the memory of his mother, Monica, followed Augustine through many years of flagrant sin, and at last turned him to the Gospel of Christ. Such was his zeal and the force of his nature that he has had an influence upon the Christian Church in every century.

Talent and bravery have been regarded as the crowning glories of man. To return from the field of battle wearing the wreath of victory; to influence men by the power of eloquence in the senate house; to search the secret chambers of Nature, and gather the rich spoils of science—for these have men dared all dangers, and searched all climes. But woman's walk is in the quieter sphere of homely duties, where the moral nature is more directly exercised. Grace is the glory of a woman; a true and fervent spirit is her crown of glory. Hers it has been, not with showy words, to debate points of theology, or engage in empty controversy, but with deep instinctive feeling to seize the truth and hold it fast. It has not been her lot in field of battle to face the armed bands, but by holy patience to live the truth, and render herself a living sacrifice to its power. The wise man, in describing the virtuous woman, saith: "She openeth her mouth with wisdom; and in her tongue is the law of kindness."

It was a true, though bitter remark of Napoleon—"What France most needs is mothers." What the Church most needs—for her purity, for her extension, for the maintenance of a warm and holy spirit throughout all her branches—is not new orders of the ministry, but "elect ladies," who, when Doctors of Divinity are quarrelling about doctrine, will live the life of Christ, and with their children be found walking in the truth.

To be an elect lady is no small honour, and one not gained without much sacrifice. It is peculiarly the race to be run with patience. In the girl it is a turning from the frivolous to the useful and the good. In the young woman it is marked by pious principle and self-respect. As the woman, she bendeth before the beauty of holiness, and above all her jewels esteemeth the ornament of a meek and quiet spirit. Multitudes have thus, through faith and patience, inherited the promises. Home is peculiarly woman's sphere, and there she will find her work, her usefulness, and her true nobility.

Here also is her danger. Her difficulty lies in the necessity of being at once not slothful in business, and fervent in spirit, serving the Lord. To serve, and, if need be, serve much, and not be cumbered about much serving; to attend to many things, and not be sinfully troubled and careful about many things; to be a Martha in diligence, and yet a Mary—not forgetful of better things. This is the Christian woman's danger. In the cares of a wife, or a mother, there is the temptation to grow bustling and worldly, to forget the keeping of her heart, to grow self-satisfied and captious about others. All work should be pervaded by the Spirit of Christ, and all cares carried to the throne of grace. It is the woman who openeth her mouth in wisdom, and in whose tongue is the law of kindness, who receiveth the blessing. Let all in ministering to their households look steadfastly to Him who came not to be ministered unto, but to minister, and to give His life a ransom for many.

From the day of John the Apostle till our day the world and the Church have been lifted up by pious and noble women. I have just got tidings from San Francisco of the death of one of the best and bravest women I ever knew. She was not unknown to this congregation. She frequently worshipped in this Church with her husband—my friend, James Scobie—when they were on their periodical visits to their native land. Those of you who have met her in private know something of her genuine goodness; but you do not know the story of her life, which I will now attempt to tell. James Scobie, when I knew him first in the early sixties, was a gold miner in British Columbia. An "honest miner" he was emphatically. Easy and free in his manner, he was strict in his observance of Sunday, in his attendance upon worship where it was possible, and in his dealings with those around him. The lessons received from a pious mother and a grave, sagacious father were never forgotten. Out in the Caribboo camp, when others on the Sunday were washing their clothes, baking their bread, and gambling, he retired to the mountain solitude to meditate, to pray, and to sing the Psalms, for which he had a special liking. "I to the hills will lift mine eyes" was a great favourite, and was literally true. The eyes were often wet with tears when he thought of home and the old kirk in Blackford. The mines were not immediately successful; and almost broken but honest, he made his way to San Francisco. He had been a mason; and there it was found that he was one of the few men who could build "brigs." From being an employee, he soon became foreman of the gang, and shortly after a contractor; and when the first railway was being put across the Continent of America, he had some of the difficult work in the Sierra range.

Having cleared some money from these, he made a run home to Scotland to see his parents and his native land. Travelling to Perth, he met Jeanie Ross in a railway carriage.

Her modest and gentle manner made a deep impression upon him. Taking her aside on the platform he said—"I want to get your address. I want to see you again, and, if I can, to get you to be my wife." The address was in Aberdeen, and from the Granite City he brought his wife in due time to Truckee. Never was man more fortunate in his wooing. Had he been advised by all the philosophers, he could not have got a wife that was better fitted for him or the position she was to fill. Truckee was then a rough mountain place, but she had the greatest interest in her surroundings, and a blessed influence upon its mixed population. She proved withal a most excellent counsellor in all his great undertakings.

The Central Pacific was finished, but other roads were opened up, in which Mr. Scobie had large contracts; and in their movable railroad camp life in California, Nevada, Utah, Arizona, and Oregon, her influence increased with growing power and wealth. She was the friend, and urged her husband to be the friend, of all the small struggling churches in these early days, and of all who were unfortunate and setting themselves at better things. After I left, they joined the church of Dr. Gibson in San Francisco (U.P.) Wherever they were the collection days were always remembered, and the people there could always depend upon the substantial aid of my friend Scobie, who became a trustee.

In 1886, they were in camp near Mount Shasta, on the Sacramento. The site of their camp is now the City of Dunsmuir, in the Southern Pacific, between San Francisco and Portland. It was my privilege to visit them there. They had a beautiful and commodious tent prepared for the Scotch minister. There I rested for a week, and in that sweet resting-place wrote articles for the *Scotsman* and for some magazines with which I had a connection. In the afternoons I visited with Scobie the workmen engaged upon the culverts and bridges on the line. There were about a thousand men under his command at the time. The monthly pay for all these had to be brought up from San Francisco. This was regularly done by Mrs. Scobie. It was a work of great danger. A man could not have done it so securely. She was well known and much beloved, so that even rough men respected and feared her. In that out-lying camp they had often to seek sleep when 40,000 dollars were around them. I will never forget my experience there. It was pleasant to have prayers amid the giant trees, and, having sought the protection of God, to retire to the neighbouring tent, with the waters of the head Sacramento making sweet lullaby.

One morning I was called from my camp study. An Indian woman had come with her sick boy. In their stores they had medicines as well as provisions. All that the Indian could say was "Scobie woman, good woman. Indian tenas man [small boy] sick." We held a council over the "tenas man." We administered castor-oil, and next day some quinine. The result could not have been better if the whole Faculty of Physicians had been there. I have often thought of that exclamation—"Scobie woman, good woman."

In a year after, they were on their way to Jerusalem. Scobie had cherished always the desire to see "the stanes o' Jerusalem." They and their daughter, Marguerite (now the wife of Professor Davies, of Princeton), left us in March, and returned to us when we were on holiday on the Ayrshire coast.

Last summer I again saw them in San Francisco. They were in their great mansion, which they had built after the toil of many years. Everything within it was perfect. The beautiful carriage and the splendid chargers were at the door every day, ready to go to the Golden Gate, or wherever else might be desired. But, in the inscrutable providence of God, the mistress of the mansion was not able to take her place in it. My wife and I had little heart to go where she went not. A sweet month we spent with her, and parted—not without a fear of the future. And now the end has come. Yet not the end, for the saintly spirit goes on to yet richer experiences. Her work was well done, and she yet speaks to us and to many others. She has left a noble record of good works, cherished in the memory of many a lonely minister—of men who have taken courage from her example, and, above all, of him who mourns his well-beloved in the far-off city. Successful in life, his greatest fortune was his wife. He spoke to her hastily at that railway station, and, after more than twenty years of sweetest intercourse, he is looking forward to the great terminus, where the scattered will be gathered, and the elect ladies will be acknowledged by the Great Master.

OLD COLLEGE CHURCH,
HIGH STREET.

ADDRESSES

GIVEN AT THE LAST MEETING OF THE CONGREGATION WITHIN THE OLD COLLEGE CHURCH, ON THE EVENING OF TUESDAY, 10TH OCTOBER, 1876.

IT is natural that to-night we should recall the history of this old Church in the past. That takes us away beyond the Reformation period, and beyond even the struggles of Wallace and Bruce, to the time when Alexander II. was reigning peacefully upon the throne of Scotland. In 1246 the Friar Preachers of the Order of St. Dominick (from the colour of their dress usually called the Black Friars), found their way into Glasgow, and began to build their Church and Monastery. Pope Innocent IV. proclaimed a forty-days' Indulgence to all who would contribute to this pious work. They were favoured by Bishop Bondington, the princely prelate of the time, who presided over Glasgow, and came to have great wealth and property. In 1301 Edward I. resided three days in the Monastery with his retinue, and left six shillings with the Friars, as remuneration for their hospitality. In 1454 the first Lord Provost of Glasgow, John Stewart, bequeathed to the Blackfriars Kirk lands and a large sum of money. In 1485 his daughter, Janet Stewart, gave similar benefactions. In the University Records, 1582, mention is made of the "Auld evidents of the Friars' manse-yeard and kirk-yeard," but these have now disappeared.

After the Reformation, Queen Mary, by a charter in 1566,

made over to the Provost, Bailies, Council, and community in Glasgow, for the support of their ministers and endowment of hospitals, the lands, houses, churches, rents, dues, and other property of the Dominicans, or Preaching Friars.

Much of this was subsequently (1572) transferred to the University, for the maintenance of a Provost, who was also to be a Professor of Theology; of two Regents and Teachers of Philosophy; and of twelve poor students.

Mr. Milne, the architect to His Majesty the King, was in Glasgow in 1638 (the year of the Great Reforming Assembly held here). He surveyed the Convent and Kirk of the Blackfriars, and declared that "the ancient building had not its parallel in all Scotland, except Whittairn, in Galloway." We are surprised at him saying this when the beautiful High Church was so near. In the pictures preserved, this old Blackfriars Kirk appears as a long, plain Gothic building.

About 1630, this Church seems to have got into serious disrepair. On condition that the town would repair it, the Church and part of the ground was disposed to the Burgh of Glasgow. The Magistrates delayed doing the work, and it is recorded that "the Church and steeple were so bruised by a thunderbolt, the same became ruinous and fell to rubbish."

Then, in 1699, the Town Council built another Church on the site of the former one, in the High Street, at a cost of £1800. But the Church had fallen on evil times in regard to architecture. It could not be said, by even the most devoted adherent, that it was without a parallel in Scotland. In one respect there were not many like it. It was a kind of round octagonal building, and had great capacity for sitters. It was a wonder to many of our forefathers that it had no pillar to support the great roof.

Until the year 1763 the professors and students attended Divine service here; but by this time the number of students had so increased that it was thought better to have worship in the common hall, conducted by a College chaplain, where the students could be more under the observation of the professors. We can scarcely realise in our day what commotion the proposal stirred up in the city. It was supposed that the professors and students regarded themselves as too good to mingle with the common folks in worship. I have a most interesting little book, published at the time, entitled, "The motives which have determined the University of Glasgow to desert the Blackfriars Kirk, and betake themselves to a chapel." It is not a bad specimen of the sarcastic. In a letter, professing to be from a professor, reasons are given for the change—some of them very curious. "We sleep, and in sleeping give no marks of our superiority; for sleeping in church is a vulgar thing, practised by the very beggars. Again, if we stay away from Church, we must either ride in the fields, or walk in College garden, or stay in our rooms. If we ride abroad, the people who observe us say we are profane. If we stay in our rooms, we must either read plays or our own systems. If we read plays, our servants whisper that we are graceless; if we read our own systems, we soon fall asleep over them, and this mars our sleeping in the night-time. Therefore, we judged it proper to deliver ourselves from all these hardships by building ourselves a chapel. The superstitious part of the town will not know whether we attend it or not."

Notwithstanding, the professors and students withdrew to the College chapel, they still continued to let those seats in Blackfriars Church in which they had a proprietary interest. This was for long a sore point with the Town Council, even so late as 1830, when, considering the increased expenses of the city ministers, they raised their stipends from £400 to £425, they excepted Blackfriars from the benefit, because the University had a portion of the sittings, and revenue therefrom, and should take its part in making up the balance to the minister. To this day the stipend of the minister of Blackfriars is £25 less than that of the other city ministers owing to this. The University afterwards sold the seats to the Council; but neither the Council nor the University thought of making up the loss to the incumbents. The connection with the University has not been a benefit to the recent ministers of Blackfriars. The Corporation have all the seats, and get all the revenue, now larger than ever, but they have not made up the difference.

THE MINISTERS.

The first Protestant minister was Mr. Robert Wilkie, who was brought from Douglas in 1621, and died in 1640. One of the most distinguished of the early ministers was Mr. James Durban. He lived in times when Prelacy and Presbyterianism were alternating. He seems to have been able to hold his own through all the changes of the period. He was inducted to this charge in 1647, and became private chaplain to King Charles and the Royal Family in 1650, and came back in the following year to be minister of the Cathedral. There is a characteristic story of him in relationship to Zachary Boyd, minister of the Barony. When that good man was making his will, his second wife, Margaret Mure, overheard him making his benefactions to the University, and approached him with the modest request that he would leave something to that "godly man, the Rev. Mr. Durban." The sententious reply was: "Na, na, Margaret. I'll lea' him what I canna keep frae him. I'll lea' him thy bonnie sel'." He married her shortly after.

Robert Craighead was the first minister of this old College Church, then newly built, from 1699 to 1711.

One of the best remembered in the city was Dr. Gillies, who filled the charge for the long period of fifty-four years—from 1742 till 1796. There still survives Robert Lang, the old doorkeeper, who was baptised by him. He was a man of fine presence and feature, and of considerable force of character. He was the friend of Whitfield, and author of "Historical Collections: illustrating the success of the Gospel," and other works. There is a description of him in Strang's "Clubs of Glasgow." His grand-daughter became Mrs. Hugh Blackburn of Killearn, and his great-grandson was the amiable Professor of Mathematics when I was a student.

The next minister was John Lockhart, D.D.: born 1760. Translated from Cambusnethan in 1796. Died in 1842, at the advanced age of 82. He was highly respected in Glasgow, and there are still spared several members of the Church who lovingly remember him.* He had three sons: John Gibson Lockhart, William Lockhart, M.P., of Milton-Lockhart, and Lawrence Lockhart, D.D., formerly minister of Inchinnan. During the later years of his ministry, he was assisted by Mr. Gibson, afterwards Dr. Gibson, a distinguished leader in the Free Church.

He was followed by Dr. M'Letchie, who was born in Maybole in 1800. Before entering into his charge here, he had acted successively as assistant to Dr. M'Leod, minister of Dundonald; as minister of Larkhall; minister of Gartsherrie; minister of the new church at Leith, built by Sir John Gladstone. In 1842 he became minister of the College Church. He attracted many by the ornate beauty of his discourses. The attendance and membership greatly in-

* They have since passed over to the majority.

creased during his ministry here, which was only for a year and a half. In 1843 he was translated to the High Church, Edinburgh, where he laboured until his death in 1866. Dr. Macrae of Hawick has published a volume of his sermons, prefaced with an interesting memoir.

The next, Peter Napier, D.D., was born in Dumbarton; He was assistant first in Port-Glasgow, and then removed to St. George's-in-the-Fields, from which he was translated to the College Church in 1844. Dr. Napier will long be remembered for the warm interest he took in the students of theology, and the great kindness he exercised towards the young ministers of the Church in Glasgow. It will be remembered by many that his distinguished cousin, Peter M'Kenzie, Editor of the *Reformer's Gazette*, was an active member of the Church, and that his still more distinguished brother, the late Robert Napier of Shandon, had his first workshop in the district. Died in March, 1865.

The last clergyman whose field of labour was the College Parish, and whose early death put an end to his quiet and unostentatious labours amongst the flock he loved so well, was the Rev. James Mackay, M.A. He was first minister of New Ardrossan. Inverkeithing, on the banks of the Forth, another dearly-loved sea-girt parish, was his next incumbency. Here he laboured for more than ten years, leaving behind him a memory sweet with fragrance, and a name that is still a cherished household word. From Inverkeithing he came to Glasgow in November, 1865. Full of vigour, energy, and hope, he entered on his work. The strain of work in the City was too great for one who, though powerful in intellect and winning in appeal, was yet fragile and delicate in frame. He quietly passed away on the 1st of February, 1873, in the 44th year of his age and in the 23rd of his ministry.

I became minister in 1873. It may interest you to state that I was a student in the University of Glasgow; that I was licensed by the Presbytery of Dunoon in 1863; that I acted as assistant to the Rev. Dr. M'Taggart of St. James's till I went abroad, as the first minister of the Church of Scotland in British Columbia, in 1865. On my return, I was called to St. David's, Kirkintilloch, in 1871. There I remained two years, until called to Blackfriars.

When we think of all these great and good men of the past, whose names we have to-night affectionately recalled; of the faithful expositions of the truth given in this place; of the members who have sat from time to time in these pews; of the prayers offered and holy resolutions made within these walls, and remember that no more will worshipping assemblies meet within it, we cannot but be deeply and solemnly impressed. There are times in life when we should make a distinct pause, and yield ourselves to the pious reflection to which the circumstances solicit us. This surely is one of these times. We are impressively reminded of an eternal past behind us and an eternal future before us. We seem to stand on the summit of one of the dividing ridges in the journey of life, and are invited to look back upon the way by which we have come and the future that opens out before us.

We look to the past. Let us remember that God requireth the past. That past is still with us. The winds travel on their courses and seem to sweep past us, but they do a work which never perishes. The sun rises and shines and sinks away again, but he leaves behind an alms-offering to the charities of fruition and sustenance which never perishes. Men are born, and live, and toil, and die, and are by *men* forgotten, but their work never perishes. It is inwrought with the present. And so also of the individual. God requireth the past. It is still ours for repentance. Opportunity has been ours. Do we look back upon opportunity embraced or opportunity neglected? Do we sadly look back upon former days that now no more return; the early days when the Almighty was yet with us in our daily prayers and our Sabbath praises? Do we feel that we have been wandering further away from God—that we are sadly soiled in the contact with the dust and heat and storms of life? As we think of what we might have been, and what we might have done, let us renew our confessions. In this solemn hour we may say, "Thou writest bitter things against me, and causest me to renew the iniquities of my youth."

The past is still ours for improvement. From failures behind us let us gather wisdom for the future. God's loving kindness is still for us. Christ still calls us on. The Spirit still invites. Like Paul, when he landed on the shore of Italy, let us thank God and take courage.

The very change which we are making is a manifestation of God's favour. He is not removing the candlestick from the midst of us. He is only placing it where the light may be more widely distributed. Though this old Church is to come down, another has already risen in its place. When Israel of old came out from Egypt, and their way was shut in at the Red Sea, God said to Moses: "Speak unto the children of Israel, that they 'go forward.'" Let us go forward in the name of God on the path which He has prepared for us. Like the Hebrews, we are conducted by a heavenly hand. Like them, we are surrounded by wonderful providences. Promises and warnings, mercies and judgments, some things to animate, and some to dishearten, come in their turn to us. Let us go forward, then, to all our joys and sorrows with brave and steadfast hearts—forward to all holy duty, to all earnest work.

In glancing at the future, let us bear in mind, that as with this Church, so to us the last night will come. As the parts of this edifice erected by the pious hands of our ancestors shall be separated and taken down, so too shall the earthly house of our tabernacle be dissolved. Many things press this consideration upon us. There are only two members of the Church who were members in Dr. Lockhart's time. Some of those who joined in Dr. Napier's time are now as trembling leaves upon the tree of life, waiting for the fall. Several admitted by Mr. Mackay have entered in with him to the joy of their Lord. Even those of us who have but a recent connection with the Church miss familiar forms in these pews. We often long for

> The touch of a vanished hand,
> And the sound of a voice that is still.

New faces, new footsteps, now surround us. Change and decay in all around we see. Can we calmly look beyond the earthly dissolution to the heavenly reparation? Are we using the world as those who are only tenants, and will require soon to leave? Are we setting our affections on those things which are above? Are we walking with Jesus, the author and finisher of our faith? Have we the assurance of our faith? Can we with Paul say, "For we know that if our earthly house of this tabernacle were dissolved, we have a building of God, an house not made with hands, eternal in the heavens?"

All sanctuaries and all ordinances are valuable only in so far as they bring us to God in Christ. If any this night are looking back upon an unprofitable, sinful past, I beseech them to remember the words: "If any man sin, we have an advocate with the Father, Jesus Christ the righteous." Once again the old voices, so often lifted up in this place, are renewed to us: "God so loved the world that He gave His only begotten Son, that whosoever believeth on Him should not perish, but have everlasting life." "And the Spirit and the bride say, Come. And let him that heareth say, Come. And let him that is athirst come. And whosoever will, let him take of the water of life freely."

After singing the hymn "Jerusalem on high," the Rev. Mr. M'Pherson added :—

This house is now very old, and yet it is not its age that is leading to its removal, but the spirit of the age.

The Church in this respect does not stand alone. One has already fallen on the north of it, and another has fallen, or is now falling, on the south of it; and now the days of this sanctuary are numbered. How many, I shall not say the individuals, but the generations that for many long years have held sweet fellowship here! But now from every stone in these walls the cry is, "Arise! let us go hence."

This house of prayer—interesting for its locality, venerable for its antiquity, and ever memorable for its hallowed associations—is soon to be levelled with the ground. In a few months, at most, not one stone of it shall be left upon another that shall not be taken down. But though this temple is to be taken down, there is a sense in which it is not to be destroyed. The candlestick is to be removed, truly, as we have heard; but then it is not in anger, not in displeasure; and though it is to be removed, the light is not to be extinguished. In a more eligible site, and in a more commanding position, is the fabric again to be raised; and even now is it rapidly rising in all its stately proportions.

And yet we cannot part with the old without a sigh. "If I forget thee, O Jerusalem!" Oh, no! My friends, forget not these—both the living and the dead—who from this place have spoken to you the good word of life; neither do you forget the good words they have severally spoken.

Could these stones cry out, to how many a faithful exposition of the Word, to how many a virtuous counsel, to how many a solemn warning, to how many a stirring appeal, could they bear witness! For here for many long years—long before even the most aged here was born—have sat the young and the old, the grave and the gay, the devout and the indifferent, the saint and the sinner, and they have passed away; and we, who are here on this the last night of its solemn history, are also passing away. It was well remarked by Mr. Somerville that not more truly shall this material temple be taken down than shall those spiritual temples—these fleshly tabernacles—all be taken down one by one. And as the Church, they shall also appear again in other forms; they shall again be gloriously fashioned. If here, like this house, they be consecrated to God's service; if here they be sanctified by God's Spirit and illumined with the light of the knowledge of the glory of God as it shines in the face of Jesus Christ; then in a fairer land, and under brighter skies, shall they appear again in much more beauteous forms.

> Those bodies that corrupted fell
>   Shall incorrupted rise;
> And mortal forms shall spring to life
>   Immortal in the skies.

And as the event itself is solemn, so is the occasion of our sitting here for the last time profoundly suggestive. *The last time!* This will be true one day of every thing we do, from the most trivial to the most sublime. The last of every thing here will come—the *last!* The last year, the last month, the last week, the last day, the last hour, the last moment, will come, and the last *word*, the last *look*, the last *sigh*. And when these have all come, death will come; and then will come infinity with its boundless expanse, and eternity with its endless realities.

"Who, then, is a faithful and wise servant, whom his lord hath made ruler over his household, to give them meat in due season? Blessed is that servant whom his lord, when he cometh, shall find so doing."

Mr. Brand, Elder, then said:—

In leaving our old Church, we are doing so with the fairest prospect of success for the Congregation. It has been admitted on all hands that the new Church at Dennistoun will be an elegant, commodious, and comfortable place of worship; and likewise, that it is the most desirable situation that could be found for one of the City Churches. Many of us will remember this old Church with much regard. Some will remember it as the place where they received their first religious impressions, "in life's morning march, when their bosoms were young;" others of us, who are more advanced in life, will remember it as the sanctuary in which we were built up in our most holy faith, by listening to the sublime doctrines, the lofty motives, and the glorious hopes of the Gospel. All of us will remember the peaceful and solemn communion seasons we have enjoyed within its walls, as well as many of the psalms and hymns, and spiritual songs, in which we united with heart and voice. A few months, it may be a few weeks, and this old grey church shall have been swept away. A few short years, and the place which now knows us shall know us no more for ever. All is change.

> Who'll press for gold each crowded street,
>   A hundred years to come?
> Who'll tread yon church with willing feet,
>   A hundred years to come?
> Pale, trembling age, and fiery youth,
> And childhood with his brow of truth,
> The rich and poor, on land and sea,

>   Where will the mighty millions be,
>   A hundred years to come?
>
>   We all within our graves shall sleep
>   A hundred years to come :
>   No living soul for us will weep
>   A hundred years to come ;
>   But other men our land will till,
>   And others then our streets will fill,
>   And other's lips will sing as gay,
>   And bright the sunshine as to-day,
>   A hundred years to come.

Knowing that we have no continuance in this life, may we act a wise and worthy part, that we may find peace to our souls at every time of review, and have good hope in the prospect of the world to come. I am sure it is the earnest desire of all present, that in the new Church in Westercraigs, Mr. Somerville will ere long be surrounded by a numerous and devoted people, ever ready to assist and encourage him in every good work.

FIFTH THOUSAND.—Reduced Price, 2 6.

GEORGE SQUARE,
GLASGOW;

AND THE LIVES OF THOSE WHOM ITS STATUES COMMEMORATE.

A BOOK FOR GLASGOW FOLK AT HOME AND ABROAD.

By THOMAS SOMERVILLE, M.A.,
BLACKFRIARS PARISH, GLASGOW.

OPINIONS OF THE PRESS.

From "THE GUIDE," December, 1891.

THE Book will be read with much interest as a genial record of the chief centre of the municipal and commercial life of the Second City of the Empire, and of the men whom the City deemed worthy to occupy a place in its "Pantheon." We share the Author's regret that the statue of Dr. Norman Macleod does not occupy a place in the Square. A series of well-executed illustrations from photographs enhances the value of the volume, which, in its printing and binding, reflects credit on our local press. We trust this volume will find its way into the hands of the rising generation. It would be a capital book for a prize in our schools.

From the "EVENING CITIZEN," 8th October, 1891.

"GEORGE SQUARE," is "a book for Glasgow folk at home and abroad." It is an eloquent, instructive, and interesting account of the Square—its history, its associations and the men of note commemorated by the statues which adorn it. This book forms an acceptable addition to the literature of historic Glasgow.

From the "GLASGOW HERALD," 1st October, 1891.

THIS is a book which Glasgow folk, both at home and abroad, will read with interest and pleasure, and will be glad to keep near them for reference. In Mr. Somerville's pages we are able to trace the history of "the Pantheon of Glasgow," from the time when it was a marsh, surrounded by meadow lands and kitchen gardens, to that which saw the raising of the splendid pile which adorns its eastern side—the Municipal Buildings. Nor does the author confine himself to the Square alone. His book embraces an account of the Tolbooth, Post Office, merchants' houses, and hotels of the olden time that led up to their modern representatives in the Square. It is excellent and most interesting reading.

From "THE MODERN CHURCH," 22nd October, 1891.

IN this volume, an account of the history and of the present aspect of the Square is followed by a series of notices of the celebrated men whose statues adorn the place, while an appropriate and good illustration of the Glasgow Municipal Buildings forms the frontispiece. The early history of George Square forms a very interesting specimen of local history; a specimen of the kind which only a city like Glasgow, large and rapidly increasing in size and importance, can afford. He handles his materials picturesquely, and his sketches are not too elaborate. As he hints in his preface, too, these lives may prove of special interest and profit to the young—a very significant recommendation. It is fresh and instructive, while the historic part has a deeper value as a permanent record of not a little that is worth preserving in the annals of the West of Scotland.

From the "SCOTTISH PULPIT," 30th September, 1891.

A COPY of "George Square," by Mr. Somerville, has come to hand. Our exclamation on receiving it was—"What a beautiful book!" The illustrations, even to the Scott monument on the cover, are beautiful. After perusal we were able to say—"What an interesting book!" It is a thoroughly good Glasgow book, presenting in short compass what every one ought to know about the city. If any of our citizens want to gratify friends at a distance, they could not do better than send them a copy of "George Square." It will be a profitable book for the young, showing how lads who played on the plainstanes before them rose to high and honourable positions. Burns and Scott are doubtless the premier articles, but all are good. James Oswald will have a new interest, too, after this, as we gaze upon his statue. Blythswood House, Sillercraig's Land, Bob Dragon's Mansion, and James Ewing's House, are among the illustrations.

From the "EVENING TIMES."

A BOOK well conceived and well executed. It tells us just what we want to know in regard to the places and the people. For example—we have an account of the origin of the names of the streets, the "Tobacco Lords of Glasgow," and other interesting subjects.

From the "EVENING NEWS," 12th November, 1891.

OF the thousands of people who pass through George Square, Glasgow, in the course of a day, few, we imagine, concern themselves with the historical significance or public importance of their surroundings. . . . These are highly interesting pages; and as Mr. Somerville brings his sketch quite up to date, readers are able to make for themselves a striking contrast between the old and the new Glasgow. The book, too, is appropriately illustrated.

*From the "STIRLING JOURNAL AND ADVERTISER,"
6th November, 1891.*

"GEORGE SQUARE, Glasgow, and the Lives of those whom its Statues commemorate," is an important addition to the history of our commercial metropolis, by the minister of Blackfriars Parish. It is certainly one of the most interesting books recently published, and we take the liberty of giving the following extracts from its pages. The extracts are headed: "Descriptions of the old houses," "James Watt and 'Beelzebub,'" "Sir Walter Scott's position in literature," "Incident in the life of Lord Clyde," "The Tobacco Lords of Glasgow," and "Birthplace of Thomas Campbell."

From the "FALKIRK HERALD," 7th October, 1891.

A HANDSOME and interesting volume, from the able pen of the minister of Blackfriars Parish, Glasgow. It is full of curious information about the city as it was in bygone times, and the story of the many changes that have occurred since what is now George Square was in a state of nature is sketched with vivid and striking effect.

From "THE COLONIST."

APART from much that is of local interest, it has really valuable contributions to the lives of Thomas Graham, the late Master of the Mint, Sir Walter Scott, and Robert Burns We did not know until we read this beautiful volume that **Sir Walter Scott** had such a close connection with the Campbells of the Saltmarket, and was distantly related to Rob Roy, whom he has made famous.

AM I MY BROTHER'S KEEPER?
AND OTHER SERMONS.
By THOMAS SOMERVILLE, M.A.,
BLACKFRIARS PARISH, GLASGOW.

OPINIONS OF THE PRESS.

From the "GLASGOW HERALD," March 1, 1895.

"AM I My Brother's Keeper? and Other Sermons," by Rev. Mr. Somerville, Blackfriars Parish. The author declares that "sermons are made for preaching, not reading; and it is seldom that those who have heard them gladly read them with much interest." We are sure, however, that the sermons in this volume will be read with much interest. They are practical and sensible; and a lively style and abundance of concrete illustrations make them easy to read, as they were interesting to listen to. The volume is closed with an interesting account of the Old College Church in High Street, of which the present Blackfriars is the successor. [Extracts made are omitted.]

From "LIFE AND WORK," March, 1895.

THESE addresses, especially the lectures, by the able minister of one of our historic parishes, will well repay reading.

From the "CITIZEN," February 5, 1895.

No apology is needed from the popular minister of Blackfriars for their appearance. They are no ordinary sermons. Every one of them deals with events of interest in the Church, in the city, or in his own not uneventful career, and altogether they betoken the cultured and largely-informed mind. Mr. Somerville, as is known, is a much-travelled man, and his observant disposition is turned to good account in these discourses. The Book is published by Mr. R. Robertson, Duke Street, Dennistoun, and is well bound. It is embellished with illustrations of the demolished and the present Blackfriars Church.

From "EASTERN BELLS," January, 1895.

THE present writer once met, in a Perthshire manse, one of the most brilliant of the younger clergy of the Church of Scotland (he is now one of the professors at Aberdeen), and he said: "Do you know Mr. Somerville of Blackfriars? I heard him preach a sermon equal to any I ever heard from Dr Macgregor of St Cuthbert's."

Mr Somerville must have many fine sermons, for the one alluded to is not included in this beautiful and attractive volume. Those selected manifest strength of thought, beauty of diction, tenderness of feeling, true eloquence, and pure pathos. A few extracts will confirm this.

From the "KILMARNOCK STANDARD," March 2, 1895.

A BOOK OF POPULAR SERMONS.—"Am I my Brother's Keeper? and Other Sermons," by the Rev. Mr. Somerville M.A., Minister of Blackfriars Parish Church, Glasgow. The author is well known as a popular and most genial minister, and also as the writer of a successful book of city reminiscences under the title of "George Square." We have here eighteen discourses and an address delivered on a special occasion—all contained in some 150 pages It will thus be seen that Mr. Somerville is far from *dreich* These sermons are brisk as well as brief—full of life and movement and incisiveness The subjects are varied; the tone is earnest; and there is a wealth of apt illustration which excites and sustains the interest of the reader, just as it must have held the attention of the audiences to which the sermons were primarily delivered. Mr. Somerville has evidently profited by a knowledge of the world and of human nature, which he brings to bear on his pulpit work with marked ability.

This extract is from a sermon on "Faith, Hope, and Charity":—
"On one of the brightest days in the Summer I went away back from the sea-shore among the hills of South Ayrshire with a friend. We wandered away up till we had left all human habitation far beneath us, and reached the mountain moor, where the cry of the plover and curlew alone broke upon the stillness; and there we came upon a beautiful spring, the fountain of the river that was winding through the valley beneath. Around the the clear and sparkling spring there grew some of the most beautiful wild-flowers to be found in the district. This text was in my mind at the time, and here, I thought, was the symbol of Charity. It is the spring of God's love rising up in the wilderness of earth. Within it and around it are the richest moral flora—long-suffering, kindness, brotherly love, humility, endurance, courtesy, gentleness; only there is this difference, 'Charity never faileth.' The late Autumn will come, and these mountain flowers will become sere and yellow; the Winter's frosts will come, and stem and petal and blossom, all will disappear; but no Autumn will ever touch the Divine Spring of Charity; no Winter's frosts will ever settle down upon its flowers and fruits. Those grand moral flora bloomed in the Paradise of God. As they bloomed in Paradise, so are they now with us; and as with us, so will they be with our children's children, for Charity shall have an endless reign."

From the "PAISLEY DAILY EXPRESS," February, 1895.

SERMONS AND LECTURES.—Rev. Thomas Somerville, minister of Blackfriars Parish, Glasgow, has, at the solicitation of friends who desired to have some of the sermons and lectures which they heard in more permanent form, issued, as a book, a selection of nineteen. After a perusal of it no one will wonder at the desire to have the discourses. As a whole, they form an excellent guide for conduct in all stations of life. They are thoughtful, earnest, and practical exhortations in simple, yet forcible language. Two of the sermons—"The Puzzle of the Poor" and "The Puzzle of the Rich"—we consider of the greatest value in these times. They are the product of an impartial and judicial mind.

From the "IRVINE PRESS, February 5, 1895.

MR. SOMERVILLE writes with wonderful vigour, making you feel that he means what he says, and that he knows what he says himself. There is no uncertainty in the truth that he proclaims; and though you may not see eye to eye with him in all that he brings before you, he leaves you convinced that he has strong faith in the veracity of what he advances. He has succeeded in expressing his sentiments in a robust and even poetic fashion.

From the "SCOTTISH WEEKLY," February 13, 1895.

A VOLUME has been issued by the Rev. Thomas Somerville, of Blackfriars Parish, Glasgow. His sermons are eminently readable, full of good, sound, healthy thinking, expressed in an eminently racy and attractive manner. His illustrations are always apposite and striking, and are drawn from wide experience, and varied and extensive reading. Nor does he fear to deal in a broad, sympathetic, and thoroughly Christian manner with the great social problems of the day. Such lectures as those on "The Puzzle of the Poor" and the Puzzle of the Rich," are full of suggestive thought. Mr. Somerville is known to readers by the sermons and articles which have appeared from his pen, in this and other magazines.

www.ingramcontent.com/pod-product-compliance
Lightning Source LLC
Chambersburg PA
CBHW020305170426
43202CB00008B/501